Confessions

of a Highland

Art Dealer

Confessions
of a Highland
Art Dealer

a journey in art, a glen and changing times

Tony Davidson

Woodwose Books

This edition first published in 2022 by Woodwose Books
www.woodwosebooks.co.uk

Chapter headings images are

cover - *The Bee Keeper*, acrylic on canvas by JAMES NEWTON ADAMS

title page - *The Return of the Light*, woodcut by PAUL BLOOMER

part I - *Swans at Clousta*, woodcut on canvas by PAUL BLOOMER

part II - *Act of Contrition*, acrylic on board by HENRY FRASER

part III - *The Web of Man*, oil on board by ROBERT POWELL

part IV - *Parallel* - linocut by ADE ADESINA

People and events in this book are recollections, memories, and sometimes these may be incorrect.

Printed and bound by CPI Group (UK) Ltd

ISBN 978-1-7396557-1-6

Dedicated to lovers, seekers and followers of
crooked paths

PART I

Composition

Opening the Door

March 1995

We drive in convoy to the church. Black Allan in a small maroon van, tilted to one side, and me in an old, almost ready-to-ditch Ford Sierra. We are like kids on bikes – practical vehicles taking us through a magical world. The old church belongs to Black Allan. I didn't question why he had it. It is just what Black Allan does. He collects neglected and wonderful things, a magpie of the mysterious. This is his hidden jewel and I am about to be stunned.

'Note,' he says with a soft Inverness accent. 'Orignal lime harling. Ornate hand-forged door furnishings, authentic but worn leaded paint and footworn Caithness flagstone.'

He removes the door chain, makes a show of finding the key, and continues his architectural chirpings.

'You will have noticed the crows, cawing a warning. This is their place. Humans are not welcome, but the sound, it adds to the atmosphere, do you not think? And you will have noticed the fine fenestration, far thinner than modern windows. It allows more light in, as does the angling of the window shelves.'

I can see the beauty of the building. It is built to be the biggest man-made structure in the community, and I can feel why it was built here too. The old waterfall is now dammed and the healing spring forgotten, but I can feel an energy that I am too young to understand. Eventually Black Allan opens the door and I can already smell old pine and dust.

'Please enter and observe the interior.'

I enter.

The church has already been disused for a generation. Once there was standing room only, every Sunday, and outside, on special ecclesiastical occasions, over a thousand gathered to hear the minister's sermon at the foot of the waterfall. They walked three miles from the village of Beauly. Now, as I walk in, it lies half-asleep, one eye open like a dolphin.

'You will have noticed the unexpected interior. Outside – classic Georgian, and inside – Gothic. Mock Gothic. Note the wooden-trefoiled shafts, unusual pink colour, herringbone roof and narrow-planked flooring. Beautifully old, don't you think? And better with the surprising interior which, indeed, dates to 1835.'

The inside is almost bare. An enormous broom with carefully painted yellow stripes and matching dustpan sit in a corner. There is an assortment of ancient chairs and Black Allan's 'magician's cabinet': cobweb-thin silk around a six-sided frame that comes to an ornate finial. It is too old to touch, an object of no conceivable modern use, but Black Allan has moved it somehow from place to place for years.

'I may, should a suitable purchaser be found,' Black Allan said, 'be in the position of allowing this fine building to change ownership. I can see that you like beautiful things.'

Beyond the church lie the hills of the west. Here it is all trees, wide-flowing river and the yellowing Scottish dusk. I am twenty-seven years old and surrounded by beauty. Black Allan is right, I realise. The Damascene awe-shine of beauty. It was beauty that pulled me from the confines of the childhood bedroom outside to the fields, towards the deer I saw in a thunderstorm from my window, and to the secret clearing in the woods. Both are now gone. The field built on and the wood felled. It lured me from university south in Edinburgh to the clear air of Inverness-shire – my body always felt lighter as it headed north in the bus – and today it brings me out to this old church. I am a moth to the light of beauty and now I am being scrutinised for a new role by the enigmatic Black Allan. He is short and bald on top, but his quick-moving eyes and limbs make him difficult to age. He also has the ability to melt away. Rules for Black Allan are a plaything. At least ten different pseudo-names help him avoid various authorities. Rumour has it that he stole slates from a construction site and then sold them back to the panicked owner the next day.

This is the murky underbelly of 1995. There is so much freedom. On a Sunday, rural pubs open in a haze of smoke, beer and pool before the community drives back for dinner. Films have captured this spirit. *Braveheart* and *Rob Roy* were released the year before, and there was a call for wild-looking extras. We came to have our teeth blackened and appear on the big screen. You could, if you wanted, exist just below the surface. Black Allan dipped up, down, and around all laws.

'Maybe we could come to some mutually agreeable solution?' Black Allan suggests.

'Aye,' I say.

But first, Black Allan plans to weigh my worth. He knows I could not afford to pay much. He will reel me in and out, part of the game of a man between surfaces. We agree to meet in his mother's house the next day.

*

The house of Black Allan's mother was a small one-bedroom cottage on the road that once went to the Kessock ferry in Inverness, before the era of the bridge. It was also where Allan lived, but there was only one bed and this was piled high with wood and old furniture. Around it were more old things: mirrors, signs and carpentry tools. The front door was jammed shut so I was shown round to the back door.

'Please mind the floor. This is my mother, Mrs MacRae.'

I stepped in, avoiding the gaps in the floor. Wet rot had taken away the first few floorboards into the cottage. Sheets of plywood were laid over the joists to make entry easier. The heat of three radiators blasted the small room where a kettle always boiled, and in this wet sauna the wallpaper curled and slipped down the wall. Mrs MacRae was bent over the stove. Like her son, she had quick eyes and rapid movements. This little cave was where she spent her time and Black Allan relaxed. Buttered bread and soup from a tin were provided. For fun, he read aloud old deeds for the church.

'ALL and WHOLE the church of the parish of Kilmorack and the whole fixture and fittings therein so far . . .'

My head dipped forward, half-asleep.

'. . . and the whole right title and interest of the Heritors of the said parish in and to the said subjects before described, and . . .'

The reading continued for a while, with delight taken in every contorted word. Nothing was too much for Mrs MacRae; even giving up her bed to bits of old furniture.

They must have slept in rota on the one comfortable armchair. Next, we had jam pieces. This was a success. Allan and I discussed possible prices for the old church and he seemed very keen for me to have it, but first he wanted to show me another property he liked. We agreed to meet at another forgotten place the next day and the test continued.

*

We drove again in convoy and soon reached the Italian sunken garden. Two once-small trees now dominated the old stairs and disappeared flowerbeds. They seemed impossibly tall. It was a place of ghosts, known only to the closest locals. We crawled through chicken wire to explore the abandoned laundry building and pondered the possibility of underground tunnels to the vanished house. Allan ran quickly on short legs, through the tall grass towards the deserted steadings, commenting on the huge clock face on the tower and how the family was so rich they controlled everything, even time. It was a visceral old place with fabric thin to other worlds. This was where he enjoyed being. Here, he was as tall as the trees, as rich as its Regency owners and as free as the river.

My next test was to accompany Black Allan to the Isle of Coll to look at Breachacha Castle. It had appeared on the market for a price Black Allan was prepared to pay and he was more than happy to elevate his life with such a grand building. But our planned arrival coincided with the intended kidnapping, drugging, blackmailing and murder of a multi-millionaire by Sacheverell de Houghton from his prison cell. In 1995, criminals thought big. Maybe this was another of Allan's pseudonyms. Either way, our trip was cancelled.

We met like spies at the fishpond in the Botanic Gardens of Inverness, which back then was free to visitors, and here we reviewed more neglected churches and marvelled at a world that once was. So many visits were made to Allan's small, run-down cottage, borrowing or returning the church's key and drinking weak milky tea, that soon Mrs MacRae began to feel like my own mother.

The summer of 1995 eventually drew to an end. I had passed my tests. More than that, I had been steeped in Black Allan's philosophy. I knew the advantages of using lime mortar. Shells are burnt and liquified before coating a building and reverting to shell once again. Cement is evil. I enjoyed the Latin names of various diseases which infect old buildings: Serpula lacrymans, dry rot, sounded almost romantic, like part of a requiem. And I appreciated craftsmanship. The old crown glass in the church was hand-blown by abnormally muscled craftsmen. Their upper bodies must have expanded to hold the glass as it was spun before it was flattened and cut to shape. In some parts of the old church it was now only millimetres thick. The chandelier hooks dated to 1835. They were too high to see but were in the form of mermaids. I was now worthy to look after the old church. Documents were to be signed at another old property the next night, and Allan set the stage.

*

It is November in Inverness. The east wind bites and darkness arrives just after 5 p.m. Black Allan has used this to full effect. The place where documents are to be signed is a large townhouse. It has a slim front, behind which lie staircases, long corridors and forgotten rooms. Inside, nothing has changed for sixty years. I am led to the front room where ancient curtains hang cobweb-like from massive ebony poles and stuffed animals stare from under their glass domes. The only light comes from tarnished candlesticks and a roaring fire and Allan's face flickers in the firelight. How many feet has it taken to wear the carpet down to a single woollen thread, or was it just the singular steps of the long-lived stationmaster's wife who once dwelled here?

'Please, take a seat and enjoy the drawing room.'

The squat red fireside chairs are comfortable, worn

to a polish in places and deeper still in others so that the horsehair shows through. Papers are placed theatrically on the coffee table. Mrs MacRae enters silently with tea in china cups and then leaves the room, and we sign. I am now the custodian of Kilmorack Church. Black Allan opens the curtain to reveal Inverness Castle and the streetlamp-lit river below. He gestures at the wonder of it. We have walked through from a back street, along a linoleum-lined passage, to an unexpected height, four floors up. The journey through this house, to this view, is a magic trick and there are few better views in Inverness than this.

Fixing the Roof

December 1995

I move from the world of ceilidhs and under-the-surface living towards a new life. Goodbye to the smoky bars of the city, where you are either waiting for a better life or are a king of the night. I melt away from this life, just as Black Allan will soon fade from mine. My new home is the Hen House at Aigas Field Centre. Driving up, I worry that it really will be a hen house. It is small, wooden and uninsulated: my first real home, and I womb up for the winter as Aigas freezes over. It is time for a plan.

I am now the owner of an abandoned church in one of the most remote parts of Britain and I have only a few hundred pounds. But I have been shown an open door. I also have basic practical skills because under-the-surface living is practical. You fix your own car and help a short-handed joiner for a little cash if asked. Survival is a practical business. I also have an Atari computer and dot matrix printer, so letters fly out.

Dear Planning Department,

I wish to apply for planning permission to reuse the old church as an art gallery.

and

Dear artist,

I am your greatest admirer; you are a genius and I would love to exhibit your work in the Highlands' newest, most stunning, art gallery.

I have two rules: start at the top and work down. Bottom feeders don't become sharks. Rule two is to breathe life into something and then feed it. The monster created might be a gentle thing. It might feed me and others, or it might eat me. It's time to embrace the best and most true things within my grasp and the way to do this is through art, by opening a gallery. The old things of Black Allan are beautiful but becoming increasingly rare. New beauty must be made afresh.

I begin work on the old church while I await replies from the council and the artists. For the first time, I became visible to the community. It must seem as if a strange bird has arrived in Kilmorack's garden. Even if abandoned twenty-five years ago, the old church belonged to others too. More pluck than plumage, I call by the local minister. He is a vast west coast man with a voice and frame that easily filled the pulpits of Beauly and the glen. I visit on a Monday and I am told to go away. 'Some people,' he says, 'work on a Sunday.' The next day the minister turns up at my church, the old Kilmorack Church.

'Why do you no give me the doors? They're very bonny. No? Then at least the old sign. What else have you got around here... I see old Bibles. What use are they to you? Maybe I should take them now.'

The kleptomania of a well-slept and deserving man. We chat for a while in the sun and then he leaves, empty-handed.

★

Over the winter I put in electricity, counting the cost of every wire and socket, learning from a large red DIY book as I go. The same vinyl-coated manual had instructions for plumbing a toilet too, so I made plans to unblock the old spring and bring water into the church for the first time in many years. To do this the supply pipe from the spring would need to be found. I dig a hole in the right area but failed to find it. Borrowing a metal detector didn't help either. Finding a water source is an ancient problem with a time-honoured solution, and a teacher would soon arrive. I worked hard at fixing the old church, but the local farmer worked far harder. He harvested at night by the tractor's headlights and awoke before dawn. Planting, fixing and tending, the farmer had little time for small talk, just a smile as he moved from one place to another. He was a man who, like the seasons, always moved onwards. But he stopped to flush out the spring. 'Throw away the metal detector,' he told me. He had two bent wires in the back of his tractor and we dowsed together.

'Don't hold them so close. Take them apart. Raise your hands a little. You see. It always works when needed.'

This was the most practical magic I have seen. We made marks on the ground and found two buried pipes – an old one and a newer one. After this we dowsed a little closer to the church cemetery wall and marked out a power line and a phone line too. This was just part of the farmer's life, not very different from fixing the hydraulics in his tractor or the cattle trough he hoped soon to feed with the spring. Dowsing is a gift that is given to those close to the ground and with a question best answered by the earth. The next stage of fixing a spring was to pump water backwards up the pipe with a stirrup pump and then let the water flow again, bringing with it the accumulated silt and frogs – dead and alive. The old church now had electricity, water and soon a flushing toilet. I still needed to fix the sagging roof and obtain planning permission, but by now a few curious artists were showing interest and turning up at the gallery.

★

The first artist to appear at the gallery was Gerald Laing. He was prominent in Pop Art in the 1960s. Back then, he lived in a New York garret and showed alongside Andy Warhol, Robert Indiana and Roy Lichtenstein. I had known him for some years before he arrived at the church; even longer than he realised, as we'd first met eight years earlier on a remote beach in Martha's Vineyard in America. I was there on a work exchange scheme and had spent the summer barefoot in the sun on the small island, while in reciprocity an American shivered in a cold English city.

It was evening and I had decided to see how far a person could walk down the deserted beach, past cliffs and the occasional isolated beach house.

This was ten miles from the nearest town. I was twenty at the time and wore nothing but loose shorts. Three friends walked towards me dressed in blazers, collared shirts and panama hats, like Mr Ripley.

'So much in common. I'm Scottish too,' Gerald Laing told me. 'I have a castle near Inverness. I'm an artist. You must visit for tea and see my studio.'

Eight years on, as we stood outside the old church, I remembered this first meeting. His non-Scottish accent had remained with me like the whisper of a mentor: we had re-established contact back in Scotland, and I had worked for Gerald over the past three years. If he was pleased or displeased, he would say my name three times: 'Tony, Tony, Tony,' and I could conjure him by repeating this under my breath. Tony, Tony, Tony.

Initially, I was invited to nickel plate his six dragon sculptures for Bank Street Tube station in London. My job was to slowly move an anode with a sock of nickel solution over the bronze dragon until it turned silver. For three weeks in 1994, the machine peeped when working and screeched when the metal of the anode touched the sculpture. Meanwhile, Gerald would either be overjoyed (a fresh commission for four large sculptures at Twickenham rugby stadium. He ran around the garden shouting 'whoopee'), or he would be down (the London council wouldn't allow his dragons to have large erect penises). But that was not as disturbing as his sixtieth birthday, which was a week of mourning.

Time spent at Gerald's castle was formative. He loved work and would be in his studio before I arrived at 8 a.m., and he would engineer and think his way around any problem. Sculpture, I learned from Gerald, is mostly drawing, planning and construction. These things could take months before a maquette is made and, from this, an armature produced. Sculpting itself is quick and concentrated. Loud music was played, and the completed work shown to selected people. Gerald made a point of letting me see the power of sculpture – through Apollo's buttocks. Invited ladies gossiped and laughed as they entered his studio, then they breathed in, silent in the presence of Apollo's buttocks. The air became hot and rich. It was like throwing a switch. That was a good day for Gerald Laing. It was the desired effect.

He'd pulled up outside the old church in his open-top Austin 7 with his Jack Russell, Phoebus, next to him. Mathematical and practical things fascinated Gerald, so he counted the geometry of the building and marvelled at the space. It is nine metres from floor to ceiling, twenty metres long by seven metres wide and there are six classical three-foot deep windows across the front. It is, he confirms, an incredible place to exhibit work, with a play of both space and proportions, things that you cannot fake architecturally. He agreed to lend the soon-to-be gallery three bronze sculptures for its first exhibition, shaking his head and muttering 'Tony, Tony, Tony.' This time out of sympathy, for he knew how hard the art world is, and the skills needed to renovate an old building. His medieval castle near Inverness was rebuilt from unroofed stone over two years by three people: Gerald, an old man and a young lad.

★

There was still the problem of the church roof to be solved. Fixing the slates was easy. I bought a scaffold tower from Exchange and Mart for £100, and it was driven three hundred miles from England in a small solitary stack on the back of a lorry. (A few years earlier, mistaking Beauly for Beaulieu on the south coast of England, a vintage Rolls Royce arrived in a similar fashion in Beauly High Street looking for the motor museum.) The old nails of my church had rusted away in many places, so I crawled across the roof, gradually reattaching them and replacing small sections of rotten sarking board. My borrowed roof ladder was too short to reach to the scaffold tower, so I jumped the last section with a rucksack full of slates and nails on my back when going up, and lowered myself down with one hand on the way down. This was a pleasant job in the heat of 1996. In Kilmorack there is either a Mediterranean-style summer or no summer at all. I knew this well, as I had spent most of my spare time walking quickly – whomping – through the hills. One of my many odd jobs was doing this with a rucksack full of grass seed on my back, grubbing new life into damaged soil to repair the ground after telegraph poles were replaced. I remember looking to my arm once to see it disappeared under a dense shroud of midges.

A more complex problem was where the roof of the old church had dropped by a foot. Purlins are the heavy wooden beams that spread the weight of the roof, and these are kept in place by handmade wooden holders, one of which had rotted away. The Ballachulish slates weighed down on top of this and, being seven metres from the ground, work access was not easy. Luckily, Black Allan had left vast amounts of scaffolding inside the church, each piece marked with his yellow-painted stripe. I set it up like a large Meccano set, from one side of the church to the other, rising upwards until I reached the ornamental herringbone lining of the roof. This was easily dismantled to reveal a purlin end that was dusty and white where the water had rotted it away. Sunlight glinted behind the slates.

Never erect your scaffolding on an electrical cable, and always be lucky if you do. On the second day of purlin repairs the scaffolding became live, while I was on it. It buzzed a little, sparked and blew the fuse on the circuit board. My last step leaping from it was enough to cut through the cable. I felt the electricity on my legs as I leapt to the ground. The guardian spirit of Kilmorack was looking after me. I reassembled the scaffolding, without the squashed and cut electrical cable.

Almost by accident, I discovered that an acrow prop (a scaffold section that screws up and down) would steady the rotten purlin. Two acrow props could raise it slightly, and four of them combined was enough to raise the roof to its original level. I measured the dimensions of the beam end and sneaked into Gerald Laing's foundry early one morning to fabricate a protective cup for the end of the purlin from bent and welded steel. This had two wings that allowed it to be bolted to the rafter. It felt incredibly solid when the support was removed, and happy to be back to its original place. After reassembling the herringbone lining I placed a piece of wood that would fall if the roof moved again. Twenty-five years on, I look up sometimes, still expecting it to flutter down.

There were also large areas where the plaster had fallen, or where sections of pink-painted arches hovered in the air, held only by the thin horsehair added to strengthen the plaster mix. I tried fixing these with lime plaster but it didn't stick, and it cracked as it dried, so I sent plaster samples with attached pink paint to a paint enthusiast to be analysed. There were small communities of enthusiasts out there, others who knew the benefits of lime over cement, and this expert loved old paint above all things. His passion was to mix and discover new 'old ways'. He was a hands-on researcher and the last source of specialist and barely-legal paint. The results came: it was an early gypsum plaster and the pink paint a mixture of white lead paint with red lead paint. This created the rich and slightly flaked appearance. Shortly after our correspondence, the expert died of toxic exposure, and lead was coincidentally banned in all paints as well as in petrol at the same time.

I was forced to use modern paint and colour-matched it, standing next to the man at the mixing machine as he added more and more red. After a week, high on my scaffold tower, the plaster was repaired, repainted and the interior presentable.

★

The next artist to visit the gallery was Allan MacDonald. I was sanding the floor, filling the fledgling gallery's interior with clouds of sawdust. To the east, where the pulpit once stood, it made lilac, yellow and red dustbows of light, and to the west it obscured a paint-splattered human shape coming my way. Allan MacDonald was a walking palette, his romper suit wiped with yellows and oranges that in his work become suns. The blue fingerprints on his baseball cap were from loosely captured Hebridean skies and the white paint on his trainers came from foamy sea paintings. MacDonald was a few years older than me, around thirty, and a traditional churchgoing Highlander.

'I'll let you show my paintings, but maybe not on a Sunday. It's a hard game, selling art. You'll not be here long. I'll give you six months before you give up and that'll be a shame. Terrible sun this: bad for painting and bad for people.'

His skin was the pale northern type, his eyes blue, and he was better suited to colder days. He was pessimistic but also secretly joyous.

'There's a wee place I love to paint from in Torridon, and in the Cuillins too, with an amazing view from just above the road. I love this building, so beautiful. It's just a shame you'll be out of business so soon. A moonbow you say. I saw one once too.'

I couldn't help liking this newest arrival to the embryonic gallery. Where Gerald Laing had power and presence, Allan MacDonald had an honest tongue. And passion. We left the sawdust, which was as bad for his sensitive skin as the heat outside, and headed towards a beat-up van.

'I paint part-time and the rest of the time deliver locally-made wine. This is their van, almost as bad as their wine. It's undrinkable stuff. Hopefully, one day . . .' His voice trailed off. He dropped in every once in a while as preparation for the grand opening came closer and letters bounced between me and the local council.

A Matter of Faith

June 1996

Kilmorack Church has sat opposite the Kilmorack waterfalls since the eighteenth century, and even before it was built, this was a spiritual place. It is hard not to feel its charge. Wide rivers, mature trees and archaeology come together to form a Kilmorack bubble: a euphoric space. This was heightened by the warm summer of 1996. One thousand four hundred years earlier, St Columba and his followers travelled down Loch Ness, not far from here, probably in a very similar state, euphoric enough to see a monster. As I worked on the church, I saw others walk past with this wonder on their faces: the Kilmorack bubble. Maybe it was on mine too. And one of my tasks was to officially change the church's use from religion to commerce. I would need permission from the highest power of all, the Highland Council, to do this. It is a simple process. A letter is sent, money paid, and a call is made, like in a wedding: 'If anyone can show just cause why this [church] cannot [be reused] let them speak now or forever hold their peace.' And then you wait.

In the 1990s there was a reverence among some for

church traditions. The cemetery gates were respectfully closed when entering, and it was forbidden to use words like 'Dad' or 'Mum' on gravestones or even to plant live flowers by your loved ones' graves. Sundays were strictly observed by the devoted. I never met an objector, but heard things second-hand.

'I've no objection at all. Personally, I think it would be grand to see the old kirk used, but Jimmy-the-Rat up the braes was saying it was like the money changers in the temple. You know, Jesus chased them out. Personally, I think what you're doing is great.'

I also heard one person saying, 'It's a great idea and I like what you're doing, but Ian-the-Hat told me he'd rather see the building falling down. Of course that would be stupid, but y' know.'

These views seemed rare to me but there was a small anti-change group. I did hear a rumour that a member of the community council used the phrase 'over my dead body'. Very few rural churches had been repurposed at this time, even fewer with an active graveyard nearby, and the community council members were all traditional church elders. I would need to wait. You always waited for the Highland Council.

★

Meanwhile, more artists were visiting the hopeful gallery. A famous wildlife sculptor arrived with his wife. His large hands moved to illustrate how well his sculpture flows. If they weren't doing this, they smoothed his blazer and adjusted his large gold ring. He told me that selling art is the easiest thing ever.

'Shine a strong light on sculpture and they'll buy it. Don't forget to send Christmas cards to clients.'

I felt like writing this advice down. He was tall and powerful and his features full and sensuous. He would make a point of making eye contact, and his pockets were always full of dog biscuits, despite never having owned a dog.

'I have a map of all the countries my sculptures have ended up, and there's pins everywhere! They travel from all round the world to see my work. Just last week I pretended to work on a stone sculpture. I do this sometimes if it's sunny. And I sold it immediately for only . . .'

Only! That's enough to buy a small house! What an amazing sculptor, I thought, and he'll let me have work. He promised a range of beautifully patinated bronzes if planning permission was granted, and then he and his wife left, like the closing of a curtain. Then the quiet. An appreciated quiet.

The artist who lived closest to the gallery was Kirstie Cohen. I first met her and Ron in a smoky

Sunday afternoon rural pub. It was the usual thing: beer, bodhrans and talk of the hills. Rumour of a ceilidh in the neighbouring glen spread and a small troop decanted and staggered into cars for the party, including Ron and Kirstie with a small baby. Kirstie Cohen painted rich landscapes where blues and greens merged with darks and whites to form misty seas and mountains. There were never figures or man-made objects in her work. They were romantic and sublime and she was selling well. I was not the smooth-looking art dealer she expected – but the romantic and sublime doesn't require a suit and tie. She couldn't say no to lending me her work, for we were now friends.

I visited her croft studio above the gallery sometimes after working on the church. This often coincided with their early family dinner, which was often 'cheesy-beany-toasties', and I would join in and wash it down with a beer. I became Tea-time-Tony, my first Highland name.

★

In August the decision from the Highland Council came back. Planning consent was refused. My plans were in ruins and my efforts in vain. I'd also lost the £270 planning fee. Maybe there was a secret relief that I could return to under-the-surface-living. The easy familiar.

There was nothing wrong with the planners. They were just a cog in a machine, following rules, both visible and secret. This reminded me of a wild party further south. It was hosted by a town planner in his open-plan home, a converted school. He was slim and clever. It was fancy-dress party and I wore a tartan rug 'plaid-style' and painted half my face blue. The planner wore a long black vicar's frock. At midnight he ripped the frock off to reveal suspenders and a kinky top. It was a great party and he was a planner: so I found out his number and phoned.

'What? That's ridiculous,' he told me after hearing my dilemma. 'They can't refuse that. It's got to be the best possible use for a church. A gallery! What do they want? A pub, a ruin? Something smells very wrong. You could sue the Highland Council for this! You must sue them. This is appalling and corrupt. At the very least, appeal.'

I did appeal, to the Secretary of State in Edinburgh. There was a force higher than the Highland Council after all.

Visitors to the church continued while I waited again. Paul Kershaw, a wood engraver living on the Isle of Skye, appeared. He was immaculately presented. Like his wood engravings, care was taken over the smallest detail. Buttons correctly done up, shoes polished, hair in the right place. I was the opposite – buttons missing, worn walking boots, hair growing. There was a delicacy to his work, fine details cut into the end grain of wood to form a small image of a mountain or a boulder. They were devotional works that took hours of controlled breathing and cutting to make the wood-block. The printing too, on an ancient contraption, needed steady, clean hands. He showed me a range of works, framed and some unframed, in a special flawless leather folder.

I had moved from the tiny Hen House at Aigas Field Centre into a shared flat in Beauly. The Hen House was a winter let, filling the calendar before groups of tourists and schoolchildren brought the wildlife centre back to life in the spring. Beauly was the hub, a gateway to our glen, and en route to the north-west. Before the building of the Kessock Bridge in 1976, everyone passed through the village. It was the place where owners of large estates stopped to buy tweeds, meats or a six-wheeled Argocat. It was also where many tradespeople happily lived. It was a balanced place, tolerant of differences. In Beauly it didn't matter if your socks came up to your kneecaps or your toes poked out of old trainers, everyone was accepted. In the dilapidated Caledonian pub, old Archie drank his whisky with white hair combed back like a cockatiel, trying his groomed looks on the twenty-something girls. 'Whisky is good with milk in the morning,' he advised me. In the summer flowers were everywhere, and Highland dancers were bussed in on a Tuesday and a Thursday for tourists.

As the summer wore on, I ran down the stairs of my shared flat looking for the results of my appeal with increased frequency.

More artists were prepared to lend me work if the planning appeal came through. Surrealist Michael Forbes would give it the thumbs-up. I visited on a sunny day. Paddling pools were out, playthings were strewn about the garden and the insect-laden air was filled with the giggle of local children. Jane, his wife, surveyed all with a tall gin and tonic. His studio was up a steep attic ladder. It was a long space, painted grey, and had more playthings than I had as a kid: jukeboxes, boxing robots and just crazy things. A large stack of black-framed paintings had just come back from an exhibition so I could see everything. Forbes painted to soothe his anxieties, so there was a man shooing away a giant wasp with a broom, a crowd on a shrinking tuft of land as the ocean moved in, and a fox dressed as a chicken. There was a frenetic quality, a flow of prophetic thoughts. He had an active mind and a body that, if not moving, gained weight, so we paced around and explored the newly arrived bubblegum machine.

He was a local, and knew all the stories of growing up around Beauly: tales of the local kids being paid to demolish a house, reducing it to rubble, or playing 'sparkies' when learning to drive. In 'sparkies' you intentionally let the wing mirror of your dad's car hit the stone along the Brahan estate road, producing sparks. He was an entertaining chap, but the world out there was a volatile place and Forbes knew it. Change would come sometime, he saw. Would the river rise and flood his house? Would his remaining hair leave him? He also painted flying dogs and fat ladies lifted by helium balloons and eating cakes from cake-trees.

★

There were now over ten brilliant and diverse artists lined up for the first exhibition, if the planning appeal were to come through. Ceramic artist Allison Weightman was also keen. She lived in the alternative community at Scoraig. Scoraig was four miles from the nearest road. To get there you had to walk from the start of Little Loch Broom or have a boat to cross the water from Dundonnell. Most of the houses were home-built without planning permission, and it had just hosted a very funky festival – the homegrown band dressed in tinfoil and smoked homegrown weed. Sadly, I missed it. And I had Suzanne Gyseman, painter of botanical drawings and fairies. There was a lot there. 'Over my dead body' is always a silly thing to say, if indeed the elder did say that. Eventually a letter popped through the post. It was a long letter, too long to read with shaking hands, but the first sentence was:

'You have been successful in your application for change of use to an art gallery.'

I couldn't read the rest. A date for the Grand Opening was set. It was to be June 20th, 1997. This was also the day the ashes of a church elder were buried behind the gallery.

The Grand Opening

June 1997

Words from the famous wildlife sculptor came back. 'Shine a strong light on sculpture and they'll buy.' This would apply to paintings too, I assumed, but I had almost run out of money and gallery lights were incredibly expensive and hard to come by. Then two great things happened. First, a small maroon van pulled up, followed by the sound of short fast legs carrying a box.

'Congratulations, Mr Davidson,' Black Allan glowed. 'You may be requiring these, and you can have them gratis and for free. A gift! Some hugely stupid people have no idea what treasures lie in their hands. Etam, the ladies' shop, was throwing these wonders out. I acquired them, so to speak. Saving them from the skip.'

A cardboard box was handed over with a wide grin. It was filled with something as precious as gold. Tiny black lights glinted. Professional display lights, chipped but discreet. Black Allan had even saved the transformers so I could experiment straight away. I decided to dangle these three metres down from the roof beams on black-painted wood. They looked great but this wasn't enough. More lights were needed.

Etam was not the only place being refurbished in Inverness. The old Highland printmakers was also having a facelift, bringing it roaring into the 1990s with a new name – Art.tm – and a new look. It was a corporate makeover, the inky democratic printing presses pushed aside to make way for conceptual art, and all the old things were auctioned off. I acquired their old lights for £50 and sprayed them black to match the others. Dark colours were the ones that suited the old church: whites shone too brightly, overpowering the natural colours. A set of gallery rules was being formed.

And how to show ceramics? I loved the natural look of hessian, and it was a major Scottish export, especially around Dundee, but that was a century ago. Jam, Jute and Journalism, they once said. I wanted a large roll so I could use it freely. I found the last jute factory, in Kirriemuir, and they kept one machine aside for hessian out of nostalgia rather than economics. Apparently not many young guys pulled up outside the nineteenth-century factory, J & D Wilkie, in search of an increasingly unfashionable product. To one side of the factory lay the past, the old creaking machine making a product used only for carpet backing, and to the right was the future. Big, bright machines, computers and new high-tech fabrics. The buzz of brains thinking about how to adapt to a changing world was as loud as the new machines . . . but not as loud as the old one. I left with a large donated roll that filled my Ford Sierra with dusty flax particles as I drove north.

There were so many paintings that I had to build additional screens to accommodate them. This was done by screwing together lightweight frames from wood and wrapping them in the newly acquired hessian. They were terrible: almost transparent because so little material was used, and they billowed when a draught caught them or dented if a painting was heavy. A long desk was made from two old doors with plywood bent to form a curved u-shape. On top of this sat an old computer given to me by one of my brothers. There was a central arrangement for wood and ceramics. More hessian was used to cover sheets of plywood that sat on two x-shapes, also of plywood, that slotted together to form legs. On top of this sat more boxes covered in hessian to raise the ceramics and wood up. I made use of everything. The church contained a congregation's worth of old Bibles, so I piled these up and put bronze maquettes on top of them.

James Hawkins agreed to lend Kilmorack Gallery works for the inaugural show too, and he arrived with these action-painted landscapes in the back of his top-of-the-range Volvo estate. It was a class act, everything fitting neatly into the car, just leaving streaks of blue paint where they glided in and out. Hawkins had been in the

Highlands since leaving London in the 1970s, and he still had a London accent and the stocky frame of Oliver Reed's Bill Sikes. But he glowered less and had adapted to Highland life, growing vegetables, hiking through hills and capturing the landscape in a vivid new way. A drum kit sat in his studio and he played this manically before approaching an array of paints, pre-potted, ready for applying to his canvases with all sorts of tools. It was about the energy, and he was capturing something. For too long Scottish landscape painting was brown, soft and misty. James Hawkins brought it up to date.

Two hundred and twenty invites were sent out to local art buyers on handwritten envelopes because I couldn't get the printer to work. This seemed like an incredible number to me, and it is, if you handwrite the envelopes. The names were compiled from artists' suggestions and included all the local players in the art world and owners of large houses. My father, a neurologist in Dundee, offered to buy wine for the opening. He thought it would be around six bottles. I ordered six crates and shocked him with the bill. Glasses were borrowed from the local hotel, topped up with a donation of Shell garage glasses that stood unclaimed in the local garage. I discovered that there were dead spiders in many of these and discreetly dusted them away during the opening.

A young student agreed to sing Carpenters songs:

'Why do birds suddenly appear, every time you are near? Just like me, they long to be close to you', backed by her music teacher on electric keyboard. Work started to be hung. It was looking spectacular. Black Allan turned up with his advice and added more flourish still.

'That's looking great, Tony. But you need a little more. You see this old chair leg.'

Bits of old wood were in the corner of the gallery, so he picked up several turned chair legs and placed them on top of my flimsy screens.

'It's like a finial. It echoes the classical architecture of the church and gives these structures more grace do you not think, and it is summer, there's life outside. Let us bring it in.'

Black Allan ran outside and gathered wildflowers: long blue borage plants and sprigs of elder. These drooped within hours but he was right. It was time to let the spirit of Kilmorack into the gallery.

I picked fresh flowers, arranged them as shown, with flourish, and put on my kilt, boots and best shirt. And awaited the first guests.

*

The preview night itself is pasted together from the comments book, stories told and flashes of recollection. This was my first encounter with the art collectors of the north and the first to enter was Shirley Ann Cumberledge. She was a lady who took control. She was in her mid-seventies and was devoted to the art world.

'I'm Shirley Ann. That's two words and no hyphen. You will be seeing more of me. Don't worry. The girls will be along soon.'

We shook hands and Shirley Ann disappeared into the gallery, into a landscape of carefully arranged hessian-clad screens with chair leg finials, wildflowers, sculpture and paintings. The closest sculpture to the door was Gerald Laing's nickel-plated bronze of *Clovis Aged Two Weeks*. It was hard not to be moved by this small, exquisite baby's head. And next to this was Gerald's rearing unicorn sculpture. Shirley Ann was in heaven. All her favourite artists were here. At the far end of the gallery was a painting of a sun by Allan MacDonald. It was so thick with oil paint that the canvas struggled under its weight.

And then the car park filled up. I was a whirr of filling wine glasses. No one seemed to notice the dead spider removal. The charismatic wood carver David Hutchison arrived wearing full Highland dress, including a feathered hat and a hugely frilled shirt. There were several tartan three-piece suits and many brown brogues. There were party dresses and carefully moussed hair, and all the time in the background was the now barely audible sound of the Carpenters.

And then cars parked anywhere they could. They packed in next to the old cemetery and lay abandoned along the grass verges of the road, with people walking to the preview in the warm sunny evening air. Shirley Ann's girls arrived. They were all ladies of a certain status. The dowager countess introduced herself. 'What is a dowager?' I enquired, as I discreeted another spider. 'It means I have moved out of the castle to make way for the younger ones and I'm very happy about it. It's good to be rid of it,' I was told with a twinkled grin. The youngest of Shirley Ann's girls was an artist. She and her husband entered the room, tall and glamorous, like the lead actors in a film. It was his ancestors who owned the Italian sunken gardens that Black Allan had taken me to, with the words 'rich enough to own time itself'. He strutted at ease, while she charmed all. 'She's not like the rest of my girls,' Shirley Ann told me, 'far too young, but we love her and she brings a little glamour to the group.' The 'group' was known as the BAGs (Balavoulin Art Group – Balavoulin was Shirley Ann's house), and her invited ladies were instructed on how to appreciate higher things. Her 'girls' were all actively attending with their tartan-trousered husbands, if they were still alive.

Black Allan and his mother appeared, and then disappeared into the crowd. This was a bringing together of worlds. It was a collection of special things in a magical space: a Brownian motion of bodies absorbing beauty. Everything was here, the surreal and the sublime, within the pink womb-like gallery's walls, moving to a soundtrack of Carpenters songs now drowned out by the ever-rising hubbub. It was not long before someone hushed the noise with a spoon tapped onto a glass, ping, ping, ping. No, no! I panicked, but it still went quiet, and there was a demand for a speech. I was forced onto a chair by Dave 'feathered hat' Hutchison. It is expected, I was told. You'll be fine. This was not in my plan! I never saw this. I was twenty-eight and more used to the intimate bench of a pub than the very public chair I was now standing on. In front of me was a sea of faces eager to let me enter their world. Like many of them I was kilted, and this was my grandfather's kilt. He wore it daily, even in Jamaica where he lived most of his life. It was a bit ripped and was thick and scratchy, but it connected me to him and to the room. By now my walking socks were at my ankles. I gave maybe the shortest and worst oration ever.

'I am not used to giving speeches, so I'll keep it short. Thank you for coming. I wish I could thank more people, but it's been a lot of work really and I did most of it myself. Thank you for coming. Shit, that is a bit short and I must thank others too.' Faces of Inverness's most economically viable looked up expectantly. 'A big thank you to the artists for letting me show their work. It wouldn't be possible without them. You, me and the artists. That's it. It's a bit short isn't it but that's always good.'

The room was still quiet, but nobody seemed to mind this short ungracious speech. Maybe it didn't matter. I was placed there to be shown and recognised, like sculpture on a plinth. I was up there to be seen and accepted as family. The crowd slowly circulated again. James Hawkins looked up in his immaculate grey suit. Maybe he could have done with a longer speech or a special mention, like they do in London.

Gerald Laing was there too. Every year he changed his wardrobe. A few years back he wore a white suit with thin stripes. This year he sported a more relaxed look: baggy Picasso trousers and an open shirt with cravat. He was talking to the only pre-gallery friend of mine to turn up, Baz from university days – or talking past him, to Baz's girlfriend – but he was impressed with the grand opening. 'Tony used to be a free-wheeling hippy,' he said, 'but now he's a capitalist like the rest of us.' He had a point. My life was soon to change. Gerald understood many things about art and life. He liked the 'free-wheeling hippy' but knew how the layers of a cake stacked. Success would mean joining a new clan. To me he just said, 'Tony, Tony, Tony, you've done it. This is an event. It will never be as busy as this again. It's incredible.'

Behind the desk built from old doors was a new red cash box and in it lay a small pile of cheques.

PART II

Colour

Dead Flies and Blood

Summer 1997

And now the daily grind of Scotland's most embryonic art dealer. The morning starts with the short drive from my shared flat in Beauly; from the thin single bed where I have nightmares that the gallery has burned down, or someone has smashed a window and stolen Gerald Laing's bronze unicorn sculpture. I am now a man with responsibilities.

There are many practical chores. I sweep the floor using a broom with a brush that is over a metre long. This task is physical and monk-like, pushing the brush hairs along the grain of wood and making little piles of dust and ingrained dirt. In the middle of the gallery there is often a mound of dead flies that have rained down from the church's roof overnight. Other wildlife is common in the gallery too: swallows attempt to build nests in the roof timbers every May, and there is the odd remnant bat and field mouse. I then walk the circuit of the gallery, adjusting labels and removing spiders' webs that hang between Bible and bronze, until I reach the desk. I turn on the second-hand computer and unknot the twisted cord on the donated magnolia phone. I am here six days a week, awaiting the unexpected.

I soon learn a rhythm. There is always warning when someone approaches the gallery. Tyres crunch on the gravel: either the quick, efficient manoeuvre of a man on a mission, or the slow berthing of a day tripper. My ear adjusts to these noises and, within a few weeks, the sounds tell everything. A scrunch of gravel and two car doors banging means a couple will enter the gallery. If there is a long delay, they have a baby. If three large cars arrive at once and there's lots of doors closing, it might be a large group of fishermen or stalkers. I treat them alike. Many faces that appear are revisits from the grand opening, bringing friends and relatives to experience the strange beast that has unexpectedly landed. Others are second-home owners, or part of the horde of amateur painters looking to learn from professional artists. Sometimes a stray soul wanders in, or the unexpectedly uplifting visitor.

The sound of Sister Petra-Clare arriving is always the same. A small car, its thin wheels cutting through the gravel, gentle door closing and the sound of soft feet. And then three short nuns dressed in habits appear at the gallery's door.

'Beautiful, beautiful. It's a blessing. I do love this painting. Allan MacDonald is so joyous in nature. Oooh. This one is beautiful too: such richness.'

Sister Petra-Clare paints icons further down the glen, in a one-nun nunnery, and this is her favourite day trip, into a space she sees as divine. She does not drive so there is always a devoted chauffeur, and often visiting sisters come too.

'Thank you, thank you. This is beautiful. I'll spread the good word. God bless you.'

Her hand expresses thoughts in circular motions as if washing badness from the air. Sister Petra-Clare does spread the word and soon monks visit too, from Pluscarden Abbey en route to their icon-painting lessons. The unsaid bond between atheist art dealer and Catholic nun gives added value to the importance of art. Art thankfully, cuts through differences.

One group of people that never arrived were those put off by a sign with the word 'Gallery' on it. It was hand-painted in a deep British Racing Green, but still the sign stood like a totem warning that, through these time-worn and hard-to-open doors, lie unintelligible things. Beware! How do you behave in a church of art? There were the creepers. They sneaked through, attempting invisibility. You might forget they were there and then, suddenly, the creeper would appear behind you, or worse still you forget about their presence completely, and start to sing along in falsetto to any music playing. To others the large gallery space was a place to perform. One client demanded that I play Bizet's 'Pearl Fishers' Duet' loud enough to shake the gallery's windows so he could bellow 'Au fond du temple saint' out as it played.

Others played out their own mini soap operas . . .

'But darrrrling. It woooould go alongside the Poussin so well.'

'Or maybe in the winter room sweetie. But we don't have two coins to rub together.'

'But it is my turn darrrrling.'

They demanded an audience and rarely bought. It was the quieter ones, I learned, that would often buy.

★

The gallery's first sales were made in the preview. The large Allan MacDonald landscape with the thick sun sold to his now ex-boss in the local winery that made such bad wine. Allan MacDonald had packed in his job and was now determined to paint full time. As the heavy canvas with the sun was loaded into the winery's rusted van, Rory, the winery owner confessed, 'You know the wine really is awful. It was my father's dream. Making local wine was his thing, not mine. The only thing worse than making the terrible stuff is trying to sell it. Can you imagine a table of this stuff in trade fairs. Never take on your father's dream: it may not fit you.'

After these wise words the rusty van drove off. Rory's passion was art, not commerce.

Another sale made at the grand opening was an exquisite Kirstie Cohen landscape. The couple who bought it arrived the next day, wanting to take it home to Inverness. At last there was a chance for me to lose my packing virginity. I didn't know many things. Bubble wrap easily rips along the trough between bubbles, for example, and parcel tape dispensing machines are dangerously sharp and should be avoided. Wrapping took all three of us around twenty minutes. It wasn't a big painting. I narrowly avoided slicing into the canvas with the steel teeth of the terrible machine, which went into me instead, so there was blood on the back of the painting. An imprint of my first sale. The sister to this painting sold too, and the bubble wrap left marks on the canvas as it sat too long in the July sun. Luckily these faded in time. Nightmares about parcel tape machines didn't fade so quickly, but gradually I learned to swiftly process a sold painting. I became efficient, like a spider wrapping a fly.

The biggest difference lay in the red cashbox. I wasn't selling large amounts, but they were large to me. One client bought a burr elm-backed chair and then, on top of this, he bought a large James Hawkins painting. On this one sale, I made over eight hundred pounds profit: more money than I'd ever had. That night, as I jostled shoulder-to-shoulder in a packed bar in Inverness, I realised that the gallery was as real and 'now' as the crowd around me. People were overjoyed to hand over a large sum of money, and they would do it again. As a free-wheeling hippy I'd rented myself out, mostly my body, at an hourly rate; now as a capitalist, I feasted or starved on my wits and how much someone was happy to pay. Gerald Laing was right. I had changed.

★

Correspondence was arriving addressed to Kilmorack Gallery, The Old Kilmorack Church. Letters were catapulted under the door where the Caithness flagstones were worn to a dip. They would get wet if not shot through far enough. Many of these were small letters on embossed Conqueror paper. 'The Lady so-and-so unfortunately cannot attend but will try later.' 'The Duke wishes to . . .', or just 'good luck!' So many took the time to write, but then letters were all there was in 1997, and the landline. Mobile phones had almost no coverage outside the town of Inverness. There was a physical chain: a letter, a handshake and eye contact – and if a sale was made, a receipt was (badly) handwritten on textured paper. The world was real. Music in the gallery, although not on vinyl, was from a compact disc. Communities were physical things. People with differences jostled along side by side. The square Lorne sausage sat beside the sirloin steak. There was even a game of shinty (similar to hockey but far more dangerous) between lairds and ghillies down the glen every August: blood, sweat and whisky flowed together. There were vast differences too. Some owned the land, some rented it, but everyone knew each other. It was a garden full of birds, from the red kite that hovered above, to the dumb but handsome grouse and the cunning tit. We shared a garden.

I was still sharing a flat in Beauly and had given its phone number to a few clients so they could contact me out of hours. This arrangement was becoming harder. I was working during the day, and then coming back to flatmates who had done little or had maybe been in the pub underneath. There was also the recurring nightmare, where the gallery was on fire or the Gerald Laing bronze unicorn was stolen. It was eventually the shared phone that drove me to move. I knew something was wrong when I entered the flat. Veitch had a smirk on his face. He was an angry man the same age as me, twenty-eight, but looked older: his face was pitted and pockmarked by dope and alcohol. He was possibly evil too, or maybe just jealous. 'She phoned and I told her, I told her that I could smell her **** from here.' The word is too crude to print here and he was proud of his little prank. The recipient was one of my favourite visitors to the gallery. She was well-spoken, one of Shirley Ann's girls. I phoned her from the gallery, apologised, and then drove to Beauly to pick up my few remaining things. Not much of my life was there: some odd bits of pasta, a duvet and a few pillows, so the move was not hard. I did not look back as I moved into my new abode, the gallery.

Sockses in Boxes

Autumn 1997

I browsed through a Sunday newspaper catalogue and ordered a futon. I could make it into a sofa in the day, hiding my night-time presence. Until its arrival, I slept on a thin foam mattress. There was a precedent: Gerald Laing's garret in New York. He told me how all the trendy artists of the 1960s slept in their studios to save money, and folded their presence away during the day to hide it from their landlords. Sister Petra-Clare, too, slept, prayed and worked in one place. It is a monastic tradition, slipped away, but not lost. It was not planned, but my life in one building was hermitic; the gallery was a cell.

I was already intimate with the interior of the old church. I knew that there was an eighteenth-century bottle of whisky hidden under the floorboards of the vestry, and that behind the nineteenth-century pink plaster lay an older, cream-coloured wall, and I knew where the roman numerals were carved into the roofbeams so that in 1796 they could be assembled more easily. But new, less tangible things are discovered when you live and sleep in a space.

The first thing I noticed was that the old church

building wasn't inert. At night it creaked as floorboards cooled down after a hot day. All sounds were amplified: a bit of rubble dislodged by a nesting bird crashes behind the wall, wind-blown particles of lime that were once bedded under the slates come down and hit the wooden floor; even the occasional rain of dead flies makes a sound as it lands: tap tap tap. There is also a climatic movement of air in such a large room. It is rare for its highest point to be the same temperature as the floor, so there is always a breeze, best detected at night from a sleeping bag on a thin foam mattress. I tried sleeping where the pulpit once stood. I thought this might be an empowered place, invested with priestly fire, but it was too exposed to the nightly breezes brought on by the church's microclimate. It was like sleeping on an exposed rock. I tried moving into the vestry, but that was also unsettling. In the vestry there were three doors and three different winds, and historically it was a thoroughfare: where the minister dressed in his vestments before walking to the pulpit. It was also where a married couples would sign the book and promised a new life. Sleeping there was like kipping in the entrance of a tomb; a lot of souls had passed by. Maybe there was something under its floor.

The perfect place to sleep was upstairs, overlooking the gallery. I had heard that in the past it was where children also slept, during long services. There was just enough space for the newly arrived futon to fit in its tiered floor, down a step like a coffin in a grave, but free from the draughts. Here I was sealed off, barefoot and undisturbed. Small lochans were always warmer than the river. I listened to Mozart's 'Lacrimosa' as I slept, and when I awoke, I washed my face in the cold spring water from the tap downstairs. If it was warm enough outside I could swim in the river for a deeper clean.

At night I would go to my coffin-like bed and read; a small light in a large room. Sometimes I strummed a guitar by candlelight. The candle's flame flickered, uplighting the gallery's plastered arch windows and making it seem as if I was in a forest. If it was not quite dark outside, the gallery's previously abstract stained glass shone inward and became an angel: the small red segments next to the round rose cross, that was now an angel's head, became its wings. The first light of dawn lit the main rose window, filling the gallery with colour. The essence of a church is light, and its worshippers were meant to find it.

I managed to construct a makeshift kitchen upstairs. This consisted of a camping stove (hidden during the day) and a sink with a tap. The water pressure was so low it could only drip a plate clean. I was worried about the smells of cooking too, so I cooked only the simplest meals: pasta, noodles and fruit. There were not many fresh green vegetables in Beauly in 1997; often only wilted broccoli and frozen peas could be found in the local greengrocer. I was not the only local on a bland diet. Lunch was far easier. Oatcakes, a food for all seasons, were eaten by the pack alongside any form of salad I could muster. Avocado and rollmop were a favourite, if I could get them. The best meal was breakfast, when the light streamed in. I could sit anywhere with a bowl between my feet and a large mug of coffee in my hand.

Most evenings were spent walking. Sometimes I scrambled down the bank opposite the gallery, crossed the dam where the waterfall once tumbled. You could walk through the woods for hours without seeing anyone, only the occasional glimpse of the gorge below. Or I would walk on the moors above Beauly. These were so vast that I never came close to finding their end on foot. Five hours' walk to the north and you would arrive in the next glen, at Orrin Reservoir. To the west, I only walked as far as Erchless Castle, once home to the Chisholm clan. But in both directions, you eventually found the sea, either coming out near the Isle of Skye, or, if you crossed more hills and the odd road, you could make your way further north and end up anywhere. Some of these routes must have been the drove roads of the past. Only ghosts followed them now.

★

The gallery had been busy and its first exhibition was a success, but I would need a second show. I had now met new people. I was an enlarged spider and my artist-catching web spread further than before. It was to the far north that I headed first, to the craft village of Balnakeil and Lotte Glob. Balnakeil faced the intensely beautiful Balnakeil Bay, and as I arrived, clean but cold winds blew over the ex-MOD base and its flotsam inhabitants. These new residents arrived from all over the world, a tough breed, seeking the peace to create things without the outside pushing in on them. If you wanted a fiddle repaired, locally made wine or a painted stone, this was the place, but it was over one hundred miles from Inverness. Lotte Glob's studio and home stood glinting at the entrance to Balnakeil. She had transformed the old barrack box into a fairy-tale house, with blue tiles and discarded ceramics set into its walls and a large pond outside. Lotte was inside. She was in her mid-fifties but looked younger. The first thing I noticed was her hands, strong and aged by clay. All potters' hands are like this. It is the cost of working at their wheel. It is hard not to notice Lotte's eyes. They are Viking-blue and playful, and her legs are powerful from time spent walking in the hills. Everything is fired in Lotte Glob's kiln: from her memories of an inspirational childhood in Denmark, to the discovery of Scotland's wilderness. It all goes into the fiery pot, rocks and things from the past, to be locked in the present.

'Tea? Would you like tea?'

I was dragged from the clean white space of her gallery and into the clay-dusted studio. My jeans picked up streaks of white powder wherever they rested.

'These are my floating stones. This is my biggest one.' Lotte sat on a large shiny round object with the ease of a yoga instructor.

'This is my smallest.' It was the size of a baby's fist.

'And this is my favourite.' This one had a glassy glaze dripping down its sides.

'I'm almost there. I need to make three hundred and thirty-three floating stones, and then, very soon, maybe next week, I will get up early, place them on the beach and wait until the tide comes in. And let the sea take them away.'

I was shocked. So much time had gone into them.

She chuckled. 'I expect to lose most of them, but most of all I would like the sea to take this one,' her favourite, 'and this one,' the largest. 'It is a way to give back. You can't offer something that is of no personal importance.'

'But why three hundred and thirty-three? Wouldn't thirty-three be easier?'

'It seems right. It is a very important number you know. Three hundred and thirty-three. I don't know why, but it is.'

We both chortled now. This number was, indeed, important and I knew it too. The deepest secrets never make sense.

She waved as I left and promised to deliver work at the gallery in time for its second exhibition. As I drove back, I pondered how there were so many factors in Lotte Glob's work – in all of creation – and they pivoted on a single number.

*

Another number was thirteen. I drove south this time, to Fort William to visit Rob Fairley at Caol Primary School. I met him in Room 13. Outside the classroom, there was a corridor of work by professional artists. Like the chairs in the infant school, the paintings were low, and if you stooped down you noticed that they were perfectly level and so were their labels: 'Kate Downie', 'Jack Knox'. Inside, a teenager was engrossed in her own work. This room was her space, somewhere young minds could express themselves, so we asked permission to remain in Room 13. It was given.

'It's not me that does this. The kids sent a letter to their favourite artists asking for work. They all said yes. Amazing eh? And they made the labels and hung the paintings.'

Rob Fairley's own work and life story was interesting,

but it was hard for him to get over the success of Room 13.

'One of their works has just been accepted into the Royal Academy in London. I've been trying to do this for years and my own work is always rejected. Would you like to see ma work then?'

He brought out a folder of fine watercolour paintings of things in his life. He loved the hills and there were detailed paintings of the snow-covered ridges around Fort William; there were paintings of objects drawn from his hermitic life alone on an island off Mallaig, where he lived as much as possible from land and sea; and there were paintings of Nepal. A young Nepalese girl had shown him, without words, her way of life. The grace of a child giving left him changed, and Room 13 was a way to empower younger people to keep this grace alive. Rob Fairley, like his paintings, was quiet and unassuming. His works expressed his love of hope, and disappointment in adults. Art can be many things, but it is best when it is giving.

★

I drove east too, onto the Black Isle to visit botanical artist Elizabeth Cameron. Everything was large: the long drive, four storeys of eighteenth-century opulence and a finely curated collection of art. The gardens were magnificent and large too. The only small thing was Elizabeth Cameron herself. She was a tiny proton of energy. By now Elizabeth Cameron was in her seventies. Her energy wasn't fading, but her eyes were, so she was unable to do many more of her famous botanical paintings. She still painted every morning though, from 9 a.m. until 1 p.m, and in the afternoons she gardened her effulgent grounds. I was whizzed downstairs to her studio in the basement. This was where she loved to be. It was less grand than above and more like a devotional cell. Botanical paintings are very particular things, she told me.

'There are clear rules to a botanical painting. The aim is to be accurate. You must show roots, seeds, buds and flowers in a way that is as scientific as possible. The art lies in finding your subjects, arranging and capturing them.'

'Wow, I love the root hairs and the way you write the plant name,' I commented. The detail was incredible. I reminded myself to look closer next time I picked a plant, as if using a microscope.

'There's no way to do that quickly. You just have to buckle down and do the work.' She moved into her store and selected six works to lend to the gallery – 'and now I must buckle down.' I was hurried out of a small door nearby. 'I must work.' She reminded me a little of Sister Petra-Clare.

★

I was now settled in my life squatting in the old church. My beat-up Ford Sierra sat parked outside at night, so most locals should have guessed I was living there, though a few might have thought I was just a hard worker. Maybe this debate was why the local policeman banged on the door. Someone had placed a wager. I answered the knock barefooted. He was not like most policemen: he was a little short, his tie down and top button loose. It was late in the day, the sky dark enough to create deep shadows under trees where the silhouettes of bats darted. It was not quite the end of his shift, so we shared a cigarette. He still had time to kill.

'Yeah, that's fine, man. Now I know you're here, I'll keep an eye out and make sure things're fine.'

He drove off looking for more action in the quiet glen. I'm sure he would have had a dram too, if offered.

★

The one thing Inverness had was a bath, in my friend Baz's house, so I was an all-too-frequent visitor to his home opposite the high walls of Inverness's prison. I was clean by six-thirty in the evening, in the pub by eight, and just as unwashed when I left early in the morning. But slowly my links with the town slipped away as I drifted more into the life of an art entrepreneur, and my gaze shifted towards the glens and, wider still, to the collectors and artists further south. I was sleeping very well inside the gallery. Once, during the second show, I lost all track of time. The previous night had been a long one, at a wedding, and Lesley, a bridesmaid, slept soundly upstairs on my futon. There was a bang on the door and a 'hello' shouted. At seven in the morning, I thought, it must be the policeman again, wanting to share a cigarette. I rushed down and opened the door wearing nothing but a towel as the day's first clients entered.

'Good afternoon. May we take a look around please?'

'Coffee?' I suggested as I flicked the lights on, ignoring my nakedness. It was now a normal gallery day: music played in the background and coffee bubbled in the cheap filter machine. Soon it would stew and turn bitter. The four visitors looked around. It was midday. But it wasn't normal. Upstairs were the sounds of a rotating and awakening girl and an occasional half-dreamed snore.

Then they started to buy paintings. 'I'll have that Hawkins and that Gyseman and why not a Cohen too?' They were all large paintings and I wrapped them fluidly (like a spider). 'Ah,' they said as Lesley appeared from upstairs, casually wearing her crumpled bridesmaid's outfit. And then they were quiet. Sadly, I never saw her again.

★

Living in the gallery over the summer was bliss, but winter was coming and there was still no heating in the building. Hope of swimming in rivers was gone.

The first signs of the coming cold were the hidden bottles of olive oil. They thickened and eventually turned yellow and solid until they could no longer be drizzled on my oatcakes. By the middle of October, puddles in the parking area froze over and, eventually, even a glass of water left in the gallery would freeze. The previous year had been unusually cold: the ground so frozen that birds landed on your hand in search of food, and if you threw snow in the air, it came down with the sound of tiny bells. As autumn arrived visitors still came, but there was a new noise as they approached; a delay. People now fetched gloves, scarves and a second coat from the back of their cars. I bought two gas heaters and put fans in the ceiling to keep the hot air down. But it got colder still. It was snowing by the time November came, and I made a new plan. Maybe closing for the winter would be good.

I moved to live downstairs in the vestry. This was impossible to make cosy, even with an electric heater. It still felt haunted by more than just winds. It was always with relief that I opened a door in the morning and stepped into the fresh air of the main gallery hall. I tried everything. I blocked off one door, and then the other. I put a carpet in, and I made a temporary wooden shutter for the window. It was impossible, just too ghostly, so I moved back into the cold hall. By now, the water from the spring occasionally froze, and I would have to wait for a thaw before the toilet would flush.

There are only three months between November and the start of February, but I visited many friends and family that winter. In November I visited a brother in Belgium, where I wandered the galleries during the day. I took an early Christmas break for much of December and squatted for two weeks in my parents' house in St Andrews, lost behind the second-hand computer, planning my next moves. In January, my stays at poor Baz's must have become unwelcome. He had a new girlfriend, less tolerant of his open house. Next winter, I vowed, I would remain open. People were wanting it. Shirley Ann had already suggested having a Christmas party for her girls.

'Of course, Tony, you can make it warm enough,' she said. 'There's always a thicker coat.'

*

Light in the gallery had a cold blue note in winter, which changed to yellow as the temperature rose in March. It was not long before I opened its doors, and cars pulled up outside once again. When I'd opened the previous year, there was an assumption that I knew a great deal about art.

'You must have been to the Slade? Where was your previous gallery?' they asked.

I replied, 'No, why? I'm just making it up as I go along. It's instinct.'

Most thought I was modest, but the truth was that I would have loved to have studied art, and maybe been an artist, but we were not allowed. If you were good at science at school, you were sent to university to gain a baccalaureate. Art was where people who could do neither languages nor science ended up. But now I was more focused, I had learned many things and the shell was hardening. The season opened without the old chair leg finials on the wobbly screens and there was little green outside to bring into the gallery.

New artists had been acquired over the winter. I persuaded sculptor Helen Denerley to lend the gallery work. 'I could let you try a few pieces, as a trial, and see how it goes, I suppose, maybe,' she suggested over the phone; and The White Tiger of the Western Paradise arrived in March. She had been working with flexible stainless steel pipe, and the tiger was both powerful from its size, and cuddly from the springiness of the flexible pipe. The same material was used to create Yggdrasil, the Norse tree of life. At its base were snakes made of brass weld and at the top of the stainless steel pipes were birds that swayed when I put the fans on. These were incredible sculptures, and they quickly found an audience at Kilmorack.

'You must do things right, artistically, or I'll whisk them away,' I was instructed by the sculptor. So I made Helen Denerley the gallery's first official bully. She was overjoyed and we had a dram to cement the deal.

Yggdrasil came close to selling to two American girls in catsuits. They must have been twenty-two, and could outflirt even an art dealer. They were hard to ignore.

'Gee, let's just get it. Put it on the card, and surprise Daddy. It could sit in the back of the Mercedes.'

They drove a large silver Mercedes convertible and it was a hood-down day. It would make an impression when they drove back to Skibo Castle, I agreed, and the doormen could carry it in, like a haggis, with the pipes playing. Sadly, they changed their mind: too hard to send home and Daddy might get upset. When the dizziness of their visit faded, I pondered different ways to send a large springy Norse tree of life to America.

*

My life upstairs on the futon was still comfortable, but people increasingly looked behind the boxes, curious to discover things, and they whispered discreetly if they found an odd sock or a neatly rolled pair of jeans. They looked under the sink and found olive oil, oatcakes and noodles. Evidence of my life began to surface. It was also tempting to take a short siesta during the day if it was quiet. If I drifted too far, I would awaken asymmetric; hair tufted and face flattened on one side. It would take ten minutes to reinflate and become presentable.

Maybe this is why some of the Highlands' elderly widows loved the gallery. They lived downsized in bungalows, the dower-houses of rural estates they might have once owned along with their husbands, twenty-years-dead colonels, majors and businessmen. They too had adapted to life alone in homes crammed with beautiful things. At night I strolled through fresh work by living artists, while they strolled through halls of memories, taking long siestas during the day, and reinflating if a guest appeared. Some were inspirational, their minds the sharpest thing on their estates. One widow lived in a converted piggery towards Loch Ness. Her dower-home had a rough cement wall with a small door when you approached, but this opened out into a glassy white space that overlooked the loch, with a rose garden below. She had purchased a painting of the twin-humped mountain Suilven, where one massif is larger than the other, like a maned head resting on its front feet.

'Suilven was once a sphinx, you know,' she told me.

'You're right, it does look a bit like a sphinx,' I replied.

'No, no. You have got me wrong. Suilven is a sphinx, but it is now resting.'

She had been in Tibet shortly after Heinrich Harrer, author of *Seven Years in Tibet,* and was told by a monk that mountains are not just sacred but alive. That the sleeping warriors, cows and sphinxes can get up at any moment, walk around and heal the world. It is not a theory compatible with plate tectonics, but dowsing had shown me how large the gaps in science were. Science was also a faith, and art was very often a science. The phone rang three times while visiting her home, and each time it was someone seeking advice. The old lady dispensed it calmly and efficiently and then put the phone down with her knobbled hands.

'Would you pick me a few roses from the garden? I'm desperate for a rose, and I find it hard to gather them now.'

I did as I was instructed and descended the steep steps, returning with a selection of blooms. I then left her flowers in a vase and her painting of a mountain on the wall. It was not long until she died. Shortly after the funeral the house was flattened by bulldozers and the rose garden buried. The estate found her pigsty house unsightly, so they erased it from memory, like so many Highland villages before.

It was already June, and this year I was not going to get caught out by winter. A promise had been made to Shirley Ann that the gallery would stay open for Christmas and that was the plan. I had solved the problem of plummeting temperatures. A temporary solution lay in two second-hand electric storage heaters, which I sprayed black and positioned as discreetly as possible, with the addition of a small propane gas heater that threw a flame across the room. This was enough to raise the indoor temperature by ten degrees centigrade and that was enough. But I would have to go as well. It was too public to live here now, too many sockses and too many boxes, and in a few months it would get colder again. It was time to move out. Before it was the Hen House. This time it was to the dog's kennel.

The Old Dog House and Soup

July 1998

I moved from the gallery into a child's painting. The old kennel had been illustrated in primary schools everywhere. In the middle of the small cottage, two metres from all sides, was a chimney on a triangular roof. There were steps up to a front door with a small window on each side. There was a path leading to the door, with trees on both sides and a small stream to the right. The neighbour had a friendly dog who liked to look into the garden. There is a Tolkien story where two frenemies enter and live their lives out in a painting, but that was me. It was a house drawn by a four-year-old.

In one miniature bedroom I piled all my books and camping equipment, and in the other my bedding. It was not quite real. The stove was from another illustrated story, black with embossed squirrels on the front and space on the hot-plate for a kettle next to a pot of soup. I fired the stove up as soon as I could to make the place homely and get rid of the musty smell, but only a slight heat came off, enough to incubate a chicken's egg. Historically, this was really the kennel worker's house. The kennel itself was the large stone building next door: with stone fireplaces and fine sandstone details around its windows. The whole of this cottage was the size of a single room and it was hidden in the darkest corner of the estate, to be unseen by dog and laird.

Instinct when moving to a new area is always to wander. It was not far to the nearest village, where a full Sunday session was in progress in one pub. It was animated with booziness, like a Hogarth painting or an Hieronymus Bosch. I gave a nod to Johnny Rocker, who was in a chair unable to get up. He was head of a notorious clan and was known as Rocker from the way he swayed after drinking. When he died, there was a trail of cigarette butts leading from a convoy of old vans to an enormous gravestone behind the gallery. We always nodded in recognition. The other pub mid-week was like a Hopper painting, empty and waiting. I would visit neither of them again.

The best exhibitions, I was told by the gallery's new official bully, Helen Denerley, needed a strong theme, and so the first two-person show was planned. Here paintings by James Hawkins would provide a wild backdrop to a menagerie of animals by Helen herself. We also planned a dance experience where a performer was to spin wolf-like around the works and occasionally jump up like a surprised deer. At one point Helen also wanted to flood the gallery so there would be reflections under her works. I would have agreed to this if it had been possible. The starting point for this show was an incredible pack of wolves which was already partially completed. The powerful bow-legged alpha male and the howling she-wolf twisted with menace. There was also a snapping youth and a male who would, if real, soon oust the old alpha. These were made from ploughshares, chains and thrown-away scrap. Hawkins was no less ambitious. His main work, *Cul Mor Reflections*, was five metres long, and took up almost the entire rear wall. This was the first of many triptychs he would produce in the following years.

Both artists were forty-four years old. It seemed a good age for an artist to be. They fizzed with energy. There was not enough light on the large triptych, Hawkins complained, so more spotlights were bought and installed. The hanging was too busy, so it was refined. Everything was moved around until it was just right. Less is more, I was instructed. A photographer was hired to make large transparencies of the show in situ, wine glasses were cleaned thoroughly, and kilt socks pulled up before the preview. Helen Denerley even made an extra piece of sculpture to hang outside on the gallery's wall: a lizard made from horseshoes, with a bolt cutter for its mouth and a car horn for its eyes. I complained about damage to the church's lime harling as it went up, but 'sometimes large wild creatures do climb the walls of old churches,'

I was told. It looked incredible and soon cars stopped to photograph the glen's new lizard, which we named Imelda after the deposed shoe-collecting Filipina dictator, toasting the sculpture and the People Power Revolution of the Philippines who ousted her, with a dram.

Word of this exhibition spread rapidly through the efficient Highland jungle drum. For a week, the press buzzed around like flies. I was reminded of Gerald Laing, who was endlessly photographed when each public sculpture was completed. He did what he was told – look right, look left, raise a hand – otherwise he ignored them. People told their guests to visit, and aging grandparents were wheeled through the gallery doors. Groups of primary school children arrived. They were brought by their art teacher, who was the same size as the children, and they stood like a miniature army in front of me, firing questions.

'Mr Davidson, why did you start an art gallery?'

'What is it like to spend so long in an old church, Mr Davidson?'

'Do you have a favourite piece in this exhibition?'

These were far better questions than the press asked. The final one, my favourite work, had been asked before many times, and it was becoming an increasingly difficult question to answer. Over the last year a transformation had taken place. My eye had moved from seeing an individual painting or sculpture to focusing on the group. It is the group that tells the story. In this exhibition, it was a tale of two artists in full strength, expressing a love of hills (James Hawkins) and animal nature (Helen Denerley), and this was made tangible with the skill of a musician: but instead of a bow, a brush was used, and a piano replaced with a welding torch. It is a chorus. It is like asking what your favourite word in a sentence is. They are all part of it, even the extra and redundant adjective.

'I like the she-wolf,' I said, 'and the snake coming out of the carved wood, and the large painting is magnificent when you see the mountain emerge from the reflections.'

The other questions, 'Why start a gallery and what is it like to spend so long here?' were profound. I did not know, and never since have known, the answer to these questions.

'The gallery just happened. It was like catching three balls: the building, art and me. And so far it has worked. It's nice being here. Beautiful things and interesting people: what could be better?'

Again, I had given an unexpectedly brief speech, even to this short and attentive audience. Afterwards, they sat or lay on their bellies, drawing, capturing a moment.

New collectors arrived too. The first of these phoned early in the morning trying to get into the gallery. Vodafone had just extended the range of mobile phones, so for the first time they worked away from the urban centres. Bad filter coffee was handed out to two brothers, their wives and friends. The wolf pack was sold to them, to be the centrepiece of a sculpture garden in the south of England. He also had a private gallery and an opera house. The following day a Norwegian shipping magnate bought a deer and a local bodhran maker acquired a large raven sculpture. Slowly most work found new homes. Helen Denerley was right, a show with a strong theme sometimes worked well.

It was now October and, with the new heaters, the gallery no longer iced over. In the kennels it was warmer too. I supplemented the antiquated stove with an electric heater and I filled holes with the corks from wine bottles where knots had fallen out of the small building's creosoted cladding. I was not the first to do this – the wall was peppered with corks.

★

I visited Leonie Gibbs in the kitchen of her and Joe's large eighteenth-century house. This was an active artistic time for her. The old Highland Print Makers where I had acquired lights for Kilmorack had just finished its rebirth as Art.tm, and the first exhibition was of Leonie's bronze sculptures and paintings. This included the *Pictish Queen*, commissioned as part of Tarbat Church's new Pictish Trail. The kitchen was both public – the door was open and people were expected to enter – and intimate. Joe and Leonie were often in dressing-gowns or eating breakfast or lunch. It was a place that existed out of time. The walls were painted a deep pink colour and the front of the room was mostly the round bow window which filled it with warm light. It was like entering the set of an Edwardian play with the sun streaming in, limelight bright. I was whisked around the house: paintings in the basement and sculpture scattered up and down Escherian stairways and left with the promise of work.

My next visit was to photographer Craig Mackay. He was dressed like a rock star with a long leather coat and a suit made by a tailor in Thailand. His commercial work was in demand for album covers and celebratory portraits, and his photographic empire was expanding rapidly, taking over the old school in Brora and, like me, acquiring a redundant church on its outskirts. His celebratory photographs were work but his real passion was the Highlands, and myths that emerged from the landscape like the gelatin silver images which formed in his baths of developing solution. They were special works, and to guard against the coming digital storm he placed a hawk's feather into sealing wax on each completed work. It was a storm we all sensed was coming.

Analogue was a hassle. If I wanted to print an image, first I would need to borrow a transparency from an artist so it could be scanned by my preferred printer. It was expensive and slow, and these precious transparencies needed to be handled with white-gloved care before they were lost in an envelope in transit. An artist's archive lay in boxes of aging acetate. The printer was like a doctor. You sat in the consultation area, on a comfy leather sofa, discussing your graphic requirement: the paper, colour and how the operation would go ahead. You might even visit the printing press too, when the work was being printed, so you could give it the thumbs-up. This world of analogue and the professionals that made it work were threatened. Next to my beige-flexed phone lay a scanner, and next to that a modem that chirped as it connected. I had also signed up to an internet server in Shetland, one of the first in the UK, and I had an email address with a long number at the end. Soon letters with embossed house names stopped arriving and digital cameras appeared in shops. The hawk's feather embedded in Craig Mackay's photograph was a talisman, warding off this new world. We were already one foot in, but not more than that.

Art remained tactile, often smelling of fresh oil paint. During the 1998 preview, this was combined with the smells of twenty different soups. Shirley Ann insisted that her girls combine their Christmas party with the gallery's preview, and better still she insisted that they cook soup for all the gallery guests. 'And the cold?' I enquired. 'Don't worry about a thing, we'll sort it,' she replied.

In truth, most of Shirley Ann's girls were young during the Second World War, and they were from families that organised life with military precision. Here, Shirley Ann was the Commander-in-Chief. Each aristocratic lady arrived exactly thirty minutes before the preview: some with a gas heater and some with tables and cloths, and all of them with a pot of homemade soup. The tall, mantis-like Griselda of Novar made a fantastic pheasant soup, the more sturdy Dowager Countess of Cromartie a fine blue stilton soup, and a pea and ham hock soup was brought by the much younger lady of the Brahan Estate. They moved cheerfully, silently, and set up their stalls under the watchful eye of Shirley Ann. There are different types of warmth: the oppressive heat of an over-hot sun, the burning heat of a metal camping mug, but this was special, brought on by the smell of soup and the sleepiness of old Calor gas heaters. There was warmth too from the short-lived, upside down-turned world that the ladies generated. Most of the gallery's regular guests had no idea that they would be served sweet carrot and ginger soup by privileged ladies, and nor did the artists who arrived to see their work hanging. It was a celebration at high tide as the sea retreated.

Shirley Ann gave a speech about how art can lift people up towards something higher. Her girls circulated among the crowd with practised ease. In four weeks' time, it would be the start of 1999. The guests eventually left and the girls folded up their tables and ebbed away to grand houses that sat more in the nineteenth century than the looming twenty-first. I headed to Beauly to have a curry with a few artists.

'That was weird but good,' Kirstie Cohen offered.

'Yes,' I agreed, 'weird but good,' and I headed back to my child-drawn cottage to slumber alone in the tiny dark bedroom.

Spaces and Faces

1999

I now had a commute: over the muddy concrete slab bridge in front of the kennels and through the scattered village of Kiltarlity. From here, just past the Black Bridge over the River Beauly, was a cottage: a building so vast compared to my kennel that it had a staircase. I would have loved to have lived here, but it was occupied by a red-headed family. I enjoyed the commute but, somehow, I belonged north of the river, near the church and the spring. It wasn't the toughness of living in the child-drawn cottage where my books had just gone mouldy, it was a feeling of an inevitable tug to the gallery. The umbilical cord could not be broken, and I knew I would return to live closer again.

The season opened with an explosion of new faces and new clans. I was friends with a South African girl with a nose stud who worked in a hidden hotel down the glen. She felt the quickening of nature and the freedom it offered after growing up in South Africa. Her mother, a member of the Dutch Reformed Church, she said, still tried to lock her in a cupboard if she left the house, even as an adult. That's all many wanted: freedom and enough silence around them to hear the quiet. The very wealthy came looking for it, some indistinguishable from each other as if they had been to the same plastic surgeon; some of them had. They had the same chin-tucks and uplifts, the same handbags and shoes and faces that looked at you, painted-on and unmoving. A few brought minders with them. The ladies brought lady-shaped shadows that tried to become invisible by sitting with their hands on their lap or standing in a remote corner of the gallery, like a trapped bird. If I offered them a coffee, their eyes would go to their lady before they shook their heads. There were powerful men with minders too.

An American general came to the glen every year to take off his medals and wear jeans and a T-shirt. It was two weeks of silence and invisibility, but the two bodyguards never left him. Both men bulged out of their green T-shirts, with apologetic faces. They knew they were not needed here. If a coffee was offered, their eyes went to the general and they shook their heads too. The General never bought from the gallery, but for him it was an adventure leaving the hidden hotel.

There were normal people too, visiting friends for the weekend, and this gave a tug back down to earth. By now the temporary kitchen was transformed into an eagle's nest where I could look down on clients and listen to conversations if they were loud enough to hear. Two girls from Glasgow summarised the art world succinctly. It was summer and their flesh oozed from summer dresses. On top was straightened hair and below was a shell of foundation-face that protected them.

'Four and a half thousand punds. That's a lot o' money Mary. For a bit o' paint on wood.'

'Aye, Morag, it's a lot. This is an affy expensive place. It's no fur the poor to buy these things.'

This was a perfect summary. I could have run downstairs and told them that it takes an artist years to find their unique voice and to perfect skills, and that prices reflect an escalator of worth. I could also have told them that artists act as a consciousness, highlighting what is important. They connect the now with deeper time. They also make a house a home and, if you are lucky, can be an investment. I could have said this and much more. But there is no argument: this is 'an affy expensive place' and it is good to be reminded. I thank them for visiting before they waddle out, sagging their small car as they get in.

In a second season it is harder to smile at comments which an aspiring art-dealer never wants to hear . . .

'How much for the bubble wrap?'

'A ladder, what do you do with a ladder?'

'Do you serve lunches?'

I heard these things daily and they normally came from people with time on their hands. It was foolish to encourage a conversation. In seconds I would know too much: what they thought of their partner, the jobs of all three of their grown-up children and the breed of dog in the back of their car. They could stay in the gallery all afternoon if fed coffee, and the deluge was hard to stop once started. Their brother paints dog portraits but only as a hobby, they fear wasps but like spiders, and their mole removal operation is due next week. Standing glassy-eyed and swaying rarely stops a monologue when you are hooked by the teller. Sometimes you must walk away – and so the free-wheeling hippie hardened into an art professional.

★

My second season needed another show with a strong theme. I had learned this last year from Helen Denerley, the official bully, and this time I would shout out to the art world: I would embrace the surrealists. It was time to enlighten people and show the psychological world beneath the landscape. I would call the exhibition 'Surrealist Tendencies in the Highlands' and I began the quest for the professionally bizarre. I already knew a few. I headed first to the River Conon to visit Michael Forbes. It was not possible to have a 'Surrealist Tendencies' exhibition without his quirky canvases. Mike was in a cheery mood and shouted down from the attic-studio window as I pulled up in the white Saab 99. I let myself in the front door and climbed the ladder to find him. He was elated.

'It's all great here. It's brilliant. Wonderful. I'm making a poster for the London Underground. Not just any poster but their millennial poster. It'll be everywhere in London next year: buses, undergrounds . . . everywhere. I'm gonna be big. I've started work. What do you think?'

He showed me a painting that was almost finished. It had all the happy Forbes elements: cakes, fruit and dogs on stilts. The only London Transport feature was a logo on the elongated cone-hat of a fat man on stilts.

'This is what people want. They like colour and dogs, something optimistic for the next millennium. I call it *A Little of What you Fancy*. What do you think?'

'That's no bad Mike.'

Round here we never get too complimentary, but I loved these new works. The centrepiece for the show was sitting there, again half finished. It was a canvas with the artist crouched inside a box, cowering from a trail of half-Bosch, half-Terry Gilliam demons. These included a floating virus, a green head with red and white-striped beaked worms coming from it, and a blue bird with a hand where its head should be. Behind this parade was a mountain, maybe Suilven. It was perfect. He promised to get it photographed professionally, and three weeks later the transparency arrived. It was used on the invitation for the surreal show, the first printed image used, other than my own drawing of the church, which I placed at the top of a vile, green-coloured leaflet. Like the chair leg finials, it was eventually replaced with the sans-serif grey and white slickness of all other galleries.

★

I visited photographer Craig Mackay again, this time in his red-painted cottage interior. He greeted me at the end of his track. Tall crow-covered trees transformed the grassy drive into a corridor. He wore a long leather coat and had a deerhound on either side of him. It was cinematic and sinister, like one of his photos.

After this I visited Lotte Glob. This time I camped on one of the lonely white beaches that scatter the north coast and fell asleep with the smell of salt in my nose and the not-too-distant crashing of waves. This is all that is needed, I thought – the drumming of rain on canvas and bare feet on cold sand. It is not much, but it is difficult to find and even harder to keep.

Lotte Glob had been expecting me. The northern drums had kept her informed of my progress.

'Your visitor tomorrow, he's pitching a tent at Ceannabeinne.'

'He's not lit a fire, and just went into his tent when it's got dark.'

'He's awake. Five-thirty in the morning. He is an early riser.'

'He's in the car and will be with you in twenty minutes.'

My second tea of the day was waiting when I arrived. Behind the studio was where experiments took place and I felt honoured to be shown into this small cerebellum. It was the most private of places, where Lotte played rather than worked. On the bench was a tower of leaflets that had been glazed and fired in her kiln, so it was now solid.

'This was an experiment. All that junk mail and what to do with it. I thought why not pile it up into a tower and see if it can be fired into a sculpture. Paper and clay mix well. It's almost there but, of course, it will never be strong enough to last. But what else am I to do with all this stuff that comes through the door?'

Next to this tower, which was level with my eyes, was a large, satanic-looking book. It lay open with a deer skull melted and emerging out of a ceramic page with the imprint of burned-away ferns around it. There were other pages and the book was bound together with black tar. It creaked if touched. She closed it to show the cover. Here was another skull, maybe a badger's, bonded into stone and clay by great heat.

'It is something I have been working on for a while. Books are fascinating. They contain things: secrets and memories, maybe answers, the lives of humans and non-humans. I can gather things from walks and fire them into pages. That's the easy part. The difficult bit is getting the book to open and close. I call this *The Book of the Dead.*'

There are not many pages because the dead things entombed within it make it fat, but this is an incredible object, both terrifying and amusing. Lotte had the childlike urge to pick up an object: stone, fern or skull, and bring it home, but they didn't go into a jar or sit on the windowsill. They were bound together with funeral fire and transformed into the permanence of stone, like a fossil, to outlive us all. On the walls of the small room were annotated photographs, scribbled numbers and formulas for glazes. I realised that this wasn't an artist's studio, it was a scientist's laboratory. It was an alchemist's lair where base elements were transformed into higher things. Stone, fire, air and water reanimated Lotte's work into being. On the wall there was a photo of a dark, leathery-looking man wearing a hat with eyes closed. The photo was from the 1950s.

'That's Tollund Man. My father was the head archaeologist of the Danish Museum when I was a girl; Tollund Man was always around.' She tells me how the bog man was in her house, on the kitchen table, and how you could see every pore on the skin of his face and the hairs on his chin too. 'It was like he was asleep. I always wanted a little leather cap like his, and he was not much taller than me. I remember his foot. It was so well-preserved it looked like yours or mine. He was both dead and alive. I was very lucky to have him in the family.'

This was the famous Danish bog body, found by peat cutters in 1950. Lotte was a small girl when her father was called in to research it. And this was a formative time, when she roamed free around the house and its large grounds, making things, thinking of her family, of what is dug up and what lasts into the future. It was a busy home, populated by the beatnik primitive CoBrA artists and musicians. Little Lotte had a lot of freedom, and now, grown up, she was not going to give up any of it.

I had been in correspondence with the chronicler of Wick, Ian Scott, and he too would be needed for a 'Surrealist Tendencies' exhibition. He now lived in New York, where he revelled in street characters and artistic parties. He captured this busy metropolitan life, and folk from Wick, with hallucinogenic detail and existential depth. He looked so far down the psychological chasm that it was often scary. Warts, spots, wrinkles and all were shown. Like everyone, Ian Scott must have been small in New York, but in Wick he was royalty. He opened galas, gave talks and hosted exhibitions in his hometown. Visiting once a year was his elixir. His Scottish paintings were stored here, in his mother's house, and so I headed to Caithness in a rented van.

The Scott family, I realised, was eccentric. There was an excitement everywhere: in talk of brother David's interest in the druggy fringes of society and about Ian's genius for seeing all souls, whether rich or poor. His mother told these yarns with glee. In this house the currency was stories, and they spilled into Ian Scott's work. I packed the paintings in the van, including a vast self-portrait in a diver's suit with a naked girl in the background, and just out of town, I was shown where their ancestors lived, the prehistoric cairns. There was a story here too, and in the fox droppings we found. Wick is rich with yarns. I was exhausted and still had not met the artist.

*

The aim of the surreal show was to light a beacon and shine Kilmorack's light further south: past Perth, past Edinburgh, to the art establishment in London. There had been a London Highland connection ever since the domestication of clan chiefs after Culloden and, after this, the Highlands had become a playground for the rich with their large sporting estates and tweeds. Very little had changed. Six-wheeled Argocats were more common than ponies now, but whisky, guns and the blood of dead animals still mingled together. There was also an army of accountants and estate agents looking to retire to large detached houses. The gallery was now known to both these worlds, and I was occasionally recognised in galleries further south too.

'You're Kilmorack,' said one gallery. 'How can you survive so far north? Let me tell you a secret. There's lots of artists out there. Once you know that, you won't be pushed around. Treat them tough. They can be replaced.'

I looked at her, quietly, in astonishment. That gallery closed a few years later. Good artists just stopped showing there.

Other galleries had far better relationships with the people they represented. The Compass in Glasgow had a surrealist tendency itself and always championed deep-looking artists. They too received parcels from Ian Scott, including the soggy remains of an 'I Love New York' iced lolly he had boxed and sent over. I was still under thirty, soft and unthreatening, and able to move around fellow galleries unchallenged. I mentioned the internet to one gallery.

'Do you think there's anything in websites for art galleries?' I asked.

'No, not at all. Maybe just as a business card, just giving an address and phone number, but nothing more than that. What would be the point? A gallery is different from other businesses.'

'You are probably right,' I lied.

The 1990s had been good for galleries. It was a time of high interest rates and million-pound bonuses. Money sloshed around and many had become used to it. As the new millennium approached, the easy money stopped coming, and these galleries struggled. A few sank into the fine port they had once offered clients, and others found that they had overspent and now owed artists money. A few gambled what was left in an attempt to make up the shortfall. For some, the twenty-first century was tumbling towards them like the backward-playing psychedelic crescendo in 'A Day in the Life'. It would reach a peak, play a note, and then fade away. I had entered the game too late to be part of this song.

★

Up north, the tune was different. Like a jigsaw, things fitted into place. Out of the blue the red-headed family left the cottage with the staircase, and I moved into it and next to the gallery. This was one of hundreds of properties owned by the Lovat Estate, and I had the blessing of the most powerful man in Beauly, the estate's factor. He governed their many properties like he owned them all, from within the steel-doored and steel-shuttered estate office.

'Aye, we could let you have that one. It is a good spot for you, but I could see if there's something more fitting, something a little grander, if you wish. We have other properties available. The cottage is, a little, basic.'

I could not understand his concern. It was a real house, not one drawn by a child. I moved into the unfurnished property with all my belongings in the back of my old white Saab. Basic is how they built cottages in the early nineteenth century. They placed large stones onto the ground and built up a wall using lime mortar and whatever stones lay around. The roof was originally made of curved branches, crucks, with turf on top. Inside lived an extended family without water or toilet. Mill Cottage was without a bathroom until the 1970s, when the crucks were removed and a second storey installed as cheaply as possible. The remains of a shed with a fireplace and a tin bath where they washed was still in the garden. Rather like the kennels, the cottage had been pushed into a discreet corner of the landscape.

Basic was still there at the turn of the twenty-first century. Cooking was on a solid fuel Rayburn which also heated the water. If it was hot enough to cook on, the hot water tank in the cupboard upstairs erupted and showered boiling water around the spare room. If the Rayburn became choked, sticky black soot rained down in the kitchen. If the fire was lit in the sitting room, a cold draught was pulled in from the front door, and if it was not lit, the same cold air would come down the chimney. There was no insulation upstairs, making it fridge-like in winter – and in the summer, it was almost worse. Windows pivoted in the middle, so they tilted into the small rooms, creating a dangerous hazard. I had to remember to weave around them or suffer terrible bruises. Blue-painted chipboard floors were upstairs and a cement floor downstairs. The garden was a weave of nettles, bramble and old fence wire. I loved it: and to celebrate moving in I purchased an inflatable sofa. It was now furnished too.

★

The gallery began to attract more devoted followers. There was Jim, a ninety-year-old ex-banker, who visited every month and bought a painting each time. He lived alone because the bank he worked for in his youth refused to give him permission to marry his girlfriend back in 1959. In those days, the bank controlled all sides of its staff's lives, and Jim had not saved enough, so now he lived alone. He wrote a letter to every artist after purchasing their work, telling them how much he enjoyed it. If I'd had to guess his age, I would have been out by twenty-five years.

People's devotion surprised me, and few more than Tirsh. Her first visit was early in the morning during October. I arrived to find a car parked outside the gallery. Inside it, obscured by steamy windows, was a sleeping figure. I crunched the gravel especially loud in irritation as I passed. People sleeping in the car park, ridiculous, I thought. A head popped out of the window.

'I wanted to get my fix of art as soon as I could. You must be Tony. I've just driven up from Stratford and would take a coffee if it was offered.'

I gave her the strongest brew possible.

'I got in about three in the morning and I'd prefer to be here than kipping in me cousin's. I come up when I can get away from the parishioners.'

'You are a minister?' She looked nothing like one: gutsy, a woman, and with a broad Black Isle accent.

'Well, a vicar.'

This became her normal route north. She would drive through the night and then sleep outside the gallery. It was either the sweet shop delight of the gallery, or more responsibility and early morning chats with her relatives, and she loved to see artists rising, changing, and reflecting the seasons.

Maybe it was the church building, with a mysterious pull built into its stones, that mades it the first place people called into with more serious problems. Often it was after visiting the hospital. They came straight here to tell their sad tales, sometimes even before going home: my husband has just had a heart attack; I have been diagnosed with cancer and have three months to live. Or maybe it was the art that attracted these confessions, because I am not an emotional man. There were more confessions in 1999. I would just give them a coffee and let the story unfold. Sometimes they looked dazed, not knowing how they arrived here in the old church in front of me. There was even a girl, maybe thirteen or fourteen, who ran in, disturbed, looking to break away from her abusive parents. They may have been outside in the graveyard. Luckily, and abnormally, there was a social worker in the gallery, and she gave clear advice on what to do, who to call and what would happen.

The abused girl had most of her life ahead of her, but some came at the very end of it. Hospice man arrived in a wheelchair with a pale face, bald but full and round. He was not much older than me, but his eyes had only the slightest light behind them. Now was the time to visit an art gallery, he thought, so he insisted on being brought here.

'Do you mind, he likes to smoke,' the nurse asked.

I provided an ashtray and she lit his cigarette. They moved like a steam train – chair, pusher and cigarette puffing as they moved around the paintings. The second cigarette was lit near a James Hawkins snowy scene of the Fisherfield hills and the third at an entangled dryad by Suzanne Gyseman. All the time he was smiling and laughing. He was ecstatic. Maybe it was the medication, or maybe he felt free in the old church, hugged by its love-laid stones, with art connecting the world of continuity to the short-lived world of now. I heard that he died later that day. He was not the only person to visit the gallery towards the end. I heard of one client who clutched a painting bought the previous week in her bed as she passed. There were others too, who visited up until the last moment, warding off the grim reaper with the vitality that art gives. It was a way of keeping alive until the last moment, and then maybe they could sneak something with them into the beyond.

*

By now Peter White had joined the gallery's stable of artists. Like his name, he had white hair, and like his work Peter White was enigmatic. He made large paintings with deep peat-like textures, out of which often came a bald-headed figure with a blend of faces – Asian, black and white – to form a universal soul, in contemplation of what is there, or what is not there. Sometimes there was a bag, a bowl, or a not-quite-empty, light-filled vessel in his work too.

'I wouldn't tell you what they're about, Tony, even if I could. I want my paintings to just be, and to let the viewer discover their own meaning. Words cloud the experience. They're a distraction, Tony.'

There was a gentleness to Peter White, and a strength that came from his scary depth. He had voyaged into another realm to make these paintings. Some artists go into the hills and come back with a picture of a mountain, but Peter White did time – forty days and forty nights in the desert – and brought back a visual statement of what he had seen.

His works looked stunning in the gallery's dark interior. They glowed silently from its walls.

*

By the time the final show of 1999 came, I had also acquired the work of ceramic sculptor Illona Morrice. I had seen her four years ago when casting bronze sculpture at Gerald Laing's castle. Illona and other sculptors arrived and discussed the casting of their work with Gerald's son, while we workers remained hidden, looking out from the dark foundry in Gerald's garage. Casting bronze sculpture was always dirty. White plaster dust was trodden around Gerald's beautiful garden and into our cars, and bronze dust gathered around my body, colouring my toes greeny-blue by the end of the day. There were the invisible welding and gas fumes too. Illona always arrived on her motorbike. When she wasn't sculpting or biking, she was rock climbing and abseiling from oil rigs. Very little scared Illona Morrice. Back then, she was in the foundry to make unique bronze figures on bicycles, but now she had moved on to sculpting large human figures in clay and elegant stoneware birds. She had moved her work outside and was enjoying the scale.

I was in the right place to see a new millennium dawn. A lot had changed since the door of the church opened for me. Black Allan appeared for the last time and assessed my progress. He arrived in the same maroon van.

'Aye, Tony, you have done well. A man of property and consequence, I believe.'

In the gallery, he nodded his approval at the improved lighting and the hefty price tags on the work, and when I showed him the cottage he beamed at its potential.

'This is very good. You have it all now. Maybe a few refinements in the cottage are in order though. I can see you here with a beautiful lady, flowers in the garden and maybe a dog.'

He then drove off and I didn't see him again. Black Allan could always vanish when he wished.

New Year was spent down the glen, by the Hen House where I had lived two years earlier. Goodbye to the old we said. I thought of the cities I had left and the friends too. And hello to the new.

PART III

Meaning

Part III

Modeling

The New Land

2000

There was no bump when the clock ticked into the new millennium. It was a cold night, and this far north it was a long wait to see the sun rise, but things had changed. At the stroke of midnight, the moderate-sized town of Inverness was declared a city. Soon after this, I received a letter from Sister Petra-Clare. All the nuns had left the glen. A long lease had expired on the Church's properties, so they were forced to become urban dwellers in Liverpool. When she left, the visits from her student icon-painters at Pluscarden Abbey stopped too. There was no more spiritual discussion with the abbot or artistic discussions with a young monk, Brother Aiden Doig. As well as religious stories, Brother Doig painted ecstatic vulva-like abstracts.

By May, the Tate Modern had opened, and a new culture of celebratory artists was crowned. Numbers were counted everywhere. How many visits at the Tate, the price of property, the earnings of a banker and the size of a city. Town life, rural life, the nuns' life and my life up until now was analogue. We absorbed things slowly.

Inverness, where not long ago there were no traffic

lights, soon became full of controls and now the streets clogged up. At roundabouts, where you were once waved on with a smile, there was now an aggressive negotiation. It was so quick that we forgot it happened.

Five million visitors went to the Tate to hang out in the Turbine Hall in its first year, buying books and pencils from the shop. Artworks were acquired on loan from bankers who had paid too much for them, but they had the money to lose. They knew what they were worth, and the Tate could not say no because it too counted things. Rents went up. Property prices went up. We could now check daily, online, and see the numbers. Nurses, doctors, patients, teachers and policemen: everything became a number that night. And a number isn't a simple thing.

Eventually, the sun rose on January 1st. I slept in a huddle on the floor and the next day put a new year into motion. First thing, I checked my email. The dial-up chirped its alien song. There was nothing in the inbox.

★

Art fairs grew and grew in the 1990s. They were lively and eccentric. Art dealers squeezed into undersized jackets or wore oversized bright green ones. They shined their shoes until they dazzled. Visitors were often the same. Goatee beards, purple robes and a harem of bangles were worn.

There were also dull, grey-suited men who rarely looked at the prices but bought everything. Art fairs had become the main feast day for many galleries, and a rich source of new collectors. I heard rumours that one dealer bought a new Land Rover with the profits of a three-day event, so I applied for London Art Fair. This wasn't accepted, but Kilmorack did get into Glasgow.

Stand 34 was a good one. To one side was Glasgow's largest gallery, Roger Billcliffe, and Roger glowered through his thick-framed round glasses when he looked towards my little white box. He would have preferred to remain within the five floors of his gallery off Sauchiehall Street. My stand was half the size of his, but three days' rental already cost a vast amount. To the other side was the Open Eye Gallery, one of Edinburgh's long-standing galleries, the city's only real rival to the Scottish Gallery. Tom had been running it for many years and now, secretly, was looking for a way out. And opposite me was Cambridge Contemporary Arts. They were based south in England, but Denise had family in Inverness, and as a student in Edinburgh I had hung out and listened to Hawkwind with her cousin's son. Before he graduated, he had an adventure with a window, a tab of acid and a hedge four storeys below. He was lucky to have survived. Denise and I were almost family.

I had an assistant on the stand, the tall, thin partner of Helen Denerley, and we had developed a tactic. I was to play good cop and he the bad one, and every deal would be sealed with a dram of Balvenie.

Client: 'Good afternoon. I quite like that Kirstie Cohen painting, the large orange one.'

Good Cop: 'Yes, it is quite nice. Kirstie Cohen is making exceedingly good work at the moment.'

Bad Cop: 'Someone else was interested in it five minutes ago, Tony, when you were wrapping the other one up. It's now or never and we can celebrate your purchase with a dram.' He picks up the bottle ready to seal the deal. 'You won't regret it, Sir.'

Good Cop: 'I'm sorry, here's a good place to write the cheque.'

Artworks and paintings flew from stand 34. Most were taken away by the purchaser, and so on each sale, the blue-carpeted avenue in front of other stands must be walked. The successful galleries walked this many times, and those who didn't sell were forced to look out from their painting-lined white cages as the victor walked past. It was not the way to make friends in this competitive zoo.

There was a banquet for dealers on the first night and I wore one of my fine shirts, purchased from the most upmarket men's shop in Inverness. I had never entered such a shop before but knew that two good shirts would turn my grandfather's old kilt into haute couture to rival the other dealers' tight jackets. In the Highlands status is often measured by how old your clothes are, not how new. The shirts were handed to me in the shop, gently and preciously, like small animals to be stroked and admired.

'Feel this one, sir. It is so soft. And I love this one too. It is from Ireland and just came over last week. It is quite rare.'

I bought a soft, thin, double-layered cotton shirt from Italy and the pre-crunched black one from Ireland. I wore one while the other dried. For the banquet, I wore the white Italian double-layered shirt and puffed my chest out in pride. It really was soft. I ascended the steps to the banquet hall.

'You cannae git in here without a jakit and tie.'

A shaven-headed, blue-tanned doorman blocked my way and I spent half an hour explaining that this was a 'look' and the shirt was expensive. Eventually, I ducked past when he was distracted by another arrival. My fellow dealers were already choosing soups. As I sat down, a glass of red wine was accidentally knocked into the lap of Bruton Gallery's owner. She was pretty angry but eventually calmed down. We shared an artist, Jane MacNeill, and she would have been happier if I wasn't there and didn't know Jane MacNeill.

When the main course arrived, I reached to get the

pepper and knocked another glass of wine over. This time it was into the lap of Will, from Will's Art Warehouse. He was a small man, an ex-jockey. Will's approach to art was less elitist than mine. His stand was full of bright, square, unframed canvases, but we also shared an artist that year, Michael Forbes, the surrealist. I remembered Mike saying 'This is what people want. They like colour and dogs, something optimistic for the next millennium. I call it *A Little of What you Fancy*.'

Will had run with Mike's thoughts and was about to set up The Affordable Art Fair. He would impose a price limit of £2,000 and would get a DJ to play music in the background. There would be bright colours, dogs and optimistic paintings in every stand. Soon there was an Affordable Art Fair in New York, and then others, from Amsterdam to Milan, and from Hong Kong to Singapore. He was a nice guy, but from another world to this hermitic Highlander. Tom from the Open Eye Gallery was there too, but he kept his pint of beer well away from my flailing hands.

The Glasgow dealers stayed at home and appeared only during the day. The ancient Cyril Gerber, already approaching ninety, moved around the fair like a friendly marionette. He was known by everyone, while Roger Billcliffe kept himself to himself. For him, the art fair was a necessary chore. He couldn't not be here, especially when he was based so nearby, so he bore it without a grin. He had learned that it was best not to say anything to competition. I had not. The gallery over from stand 34 chatted quite frequently about her cousin's son (my friend) and life in the north. I was being probed without realising.

'How is it, running a gallery so far north?' she asked, avoiding eye contact.

'It's great. You don't have the overheads of a big city gallery, and you don't have to fight over artists. If it's quiet, I can take a deckchair outside and sit in shorts sunning myself. Sometimes I put a sign up and swim in the river when it's very hot. And there are lots of good clients: best of all, some of them are prepared to spend serious money. It couldn't be better. Why?'

She must have decided right then to relocate, for she moved on from her southern gallery, bought a building overlooking Inverness Castle and opened a gallery in town within eight months.

Time and emotions are focused under the bright lights and white walls of an art fair. On day one, it is exciting. Your legs are strong. On the second day, you are glad you brought a chair. For much of the time no one strolls down your avenue of white boxes. You stand, wait and reflect. On day three, you look haggard in your un-ironed shirt. The strongest paintings have sold and the display looks diminished. On day four, the invasion comes. In Glasgow it is cheap entry day which is there to ease criticism of elitism. Mothers push prams, spotted youths stroll around in open-mouthed calf-faced gangs, and you want all of them to go and the empty stand, with its bright white light of introspection, to return. An art fair is not a natural place for a free spirit to be. It is either too high, or too low.

Finally, it came to an end. Exhibitors abandoned the vast white tent on George Square in an explosion of paintings crudely loaded into vans. It had been our home for the past four days and no one would miss it. It was a long drive. I was still wearing my grandfather's kilt. The road north was like an embrace. It welcomed me. The van felt like it was floating by the time the road dipped into Inverness. I had a wallet full of cheques and the bank teller in Beauly congratulated me when I appeared the next day, but I did not apply again. An art fair is not natural. Let them come to me.

*

While I was away, mice had made a home of the oven glove which hung next to the Rayburn. They had chewed and fluffed up its insulated interior and stacked each finger with nuts. I sat on the inflatable sofa next door in its soot-blackened interior, shot beer tins with my brother's air rifle and contemplated the profits. Bang. Smash. The profits were not vast, but they were enough to reinvest. Bang. Smash. I put down the gun. The one thing that would make the large church hall into a cosier space was a fire. It was obvious. In Scotland we all secretly long for a hearth. Even in summer, I look forward to winter coming so I can light the fire and sit by it. It defines a building, like eyes in a face, and it would redefine the gallery: taking it away from its Church of Scotland past and towards an artistic future. I knew of just the stove manufacturer to do this, in the south of Scotland, and I commissioned a large pyramid-shaped stove with a central chimney and prepared the room for installation.

Installing a stove, I discovered, involves cutting a hole in the roof, and this would need to be precise and neat because of the gallery's intricate wood-lined ceiling. I made a template from a cardboard tube cut at the roof's forty-three degree angle and dropped a plumb line to where the stove would sit. I then cut into the pristine wood. Luck was with me – the hole sat perfectly between two hidden rafters. It would have been a disaster if it had been an inch to either side. Slates were removed and the stainless steel chimney screwed into place. The hearth was simple: two large slabs of polished Caithness stone, resting on blocks. They were so heavy that the back of the Saab bounced on its tyres on the journey back from

Inverness. I fabricated a metal hanger to hold the stainless steel pipe the correct distance from the roof beam. The stove arrived on the back of a truck and I joined the final pieces of stainless steel pipe together and lit the stove. It was done, and fire was harnessed. With a new heart, the space became even more alive and people lingered around the heat. There was still a small amount of money left, so I commissioned a large round desk where the computer could sit: a brain to go with the heart. And the courage – I would have to make that. The new desk was made by artist Jane MacNeill's husband, Dougal, and was also a good height for cheques to be signed.

I had first met Jane at her postgraduate exhibition the previous year. All of her icon-like angels had sold, and she stood surrounded by glowing figures with golden halos and red dots.

'This is really quite embarrassing. It's a complete fluke. I'm sure it's a mistake and they'll come back and demand a refund. I've been offered a solo exhibition in the south too, from a nice lady who owns Bruton Gallery. It would have been good to let some more people have a painting. It doesn't seem right. I'm sure people will change their minds when they sober up.'

Jane MacNeill, like her work, was able to both fade into the background and glint forward at the same time. She was a Highlander, from Aviemore, and hoped to move north again, to be surrounded by the soft intelligent hills of her childhood. The busy streets of Edinburgh and Glasgow sat on her like borrowed clothing. There was a paradox: MacNeill painted angels and did not want to be an angel painter.

The new desk was delivered and the old one removed. Two panelled doors, the last of the hessian from the Kirriemuir jute mill and a plywood top: there wasn't much to it. Profits from Glasgow Art Fair were now gone but the gallery was more grown-up than ever. I still had the odd nightmare of suits, ties and real jobs, or long university corridors.

*

All galleries now had a computer on the desk. Most continued to write receipts in a carbon-sheeted book and used the computer for playing games: solitaire and minesweeper mostly. It was like a condiment, to be used occasionally and sparingly, but sitting there: a mountain to be climbed, and we all looked at it. Everyone had a website now, but no one knew what to do with it. I designed Kilmorack's site on pirated software and uploaded it onto the gallery's Shetland server. It was basic: pages, headers and grids that provided information should anyone ever look. On the bottom of the page was a counter that clicked slowly up into the hundreds. The temptation was there to change its design. One week the pages were white, and the next they were black or green. Like solitaire, it was a game without a purpose.

A few galleries and artists played it to an aesthetic high. They were the 'flash' websites, with mesmeric entrance pages where dots merged into the logo to the accompaniment of mood music. They were like slow-motion freeze-frame advertisements on television. Michael 'the surrealist' Forbes's website went further: heads toppled backwards and paintings spilled from the decapitated neck. There was always movement: an eye blinking or a foot tapping. Making a flash website was an addictive game. All that was required was more pirated software and time. Lots of time. I called to visit Michael Forbes. The boxing robots were pushed to the side and in their place was a computer with inbuilt neon lights.

'I've been up most of the night. It's the new world, Tony. The way of the future. You can do everything here, and it's easy when you get the hang of it.'

Michael Forbes had always been an early adopter.

'Don't you think it's wonderful, Tony? I love it. It's taken hours . . . no, days and nights. Ha ha.'

'I'm sorry, Mike. I find it a little distracting. The music and eyes always blinking, but it is clever.'

A few years later we swapped our music. It was on the

computers' hard drives anyway. He had been impressed by the smooth soul, Morricone, gospel and Bach that played in the gallery. In the old church building music was always gut-pullingly powerful – and in his studio I loved the groovy electric film tracks he played. A few weeks later and we deleted each other's music. Mine was too black and retro for Mike's taste, and his was too new for mine. Roads fork, and Michael 'the surrealist' Forbes chose a new path. Like a mirror to the world, he was less surreal now. The digital and the celebratory had taken its place.

I ploughed on with my very boring HTML website, changing colour and code. Kilmorack Gallery's website rarely got better but it always changed as I absorbed fresh digital skills. Slowly I climbed the mountain on the desk. There were professionals who could help, the full-time citizens of the wild-web-west but, like me and Michael Forbes, they were self-taught and anything they did was instantly out of date. The wild-web-west was a shanty town, or at the very most a studio set. There was little behind the façade and the doors were painted on. It was, however, a new continent, and some seeds grew. That June, as I changed background colours on Kilmorack's website, Amazon, the book website, began to offer non-books for sale, Confinity merged with a bank to form PayPal, and eBay offered new goods for sale as well as old. The virtual continent was populating and forming a hierarchy.

★

Evenings were spent exploring deeper into Mill Cottage's garden, where brambles scratched and nettles stung. The far end had the most evening sun, but to get there I needed to wear a boiler suit. Inside the cottage, what few windows and rooms existed were in the wrong places. Upstairs windows started at the ceiling so there was no space for curtains. There was potential for improvement. It started with a built-in cupboard. It was chipboard with imitation wood grain, so it had to go. I ripped it out and threw the remains outside the front door. That wasn't enough. Next, I looked at the kitchen door. It made the small room cramped, so I removed it, and then the living room door too. None of this was enough, so I removed the small wall that held the kitchen door. Better, but not enough. By dinner all the partitions downstairs sat in a pile outside the front door. The improvement was vast. The cooker now heated the whole house, and one good room was better than two boxes. I had almost forgotten that I didn't own the house. It was time to visit the estate factor to see if they would sell.

The next day I put on clean clothes and went to the bank. It was easy to get a mortgage. Self-certified ones were especially tailored to those who couldn't afford them. Next, I visited the estate office. The factor was there, the tweed-suited king bee in his shuttered office, and I was beckoned in.

'You would like to buy Mill Cottage?'

His eyebrows went up and a smile almost rose too. He must have known that most of their property's lower floor was now awaiting the next bonfire, but he said nothing.

'That might be possible.' He was thinking on his feet. 'Mill Cottage needs work, but it has potential. It is a special one. Maybe somewhere else would be better. I can show you another.'

We drove to a line of cottages not too far from Mill Cottage.

'One of these? I could let you have one of these.'

My face sagged. Why live in a rural street? It was one of a row of four cottages. He could see that it was not for me.

'OK, let's make a deal on Mill Cottage.'

The factor named a price, stuck to it, and we shook hands. Within a few weeks the deeds were transferred. By that time, I had removed everything from upstairs: floors, walls and ceiling. It was a cold bare box and I spent all winter putting it back. This time with triple-glazed windows and fat insulation everywhere. I moved the rooms around, so the spare room was a better size, and

I built doors out of spare floorboards and installed a water heater that didn't erupt like a geyser. I painted the blackened wood downstairs the same colour as the gallery, pink. It was rustic, but a real home. I tackled the sunny spot in the garden and created a patio, planted a copper beech hedge and thinned the neglected trees so they could grow stronger, and the geans on them fatter and even more tasty. The cosier the cottage became, the less the bright lights and bars of the city pulled. I had everything here.

'Do you fancy a night out, Tony?' they asked.

'I would but I've just put a baked potato in the oven,' I replied.

Rural places can be like this when you find a home.

★

The gallery showed most of the leading Highland artists. James Hawkins still outsold others, and ownership of one of his paintings, a Hawkins, was a way into an exclusive club. It signalled to the world who you were – a modern, wild hearted-man that loved mountains, a successful and tasteful person. Like Michael 'the surrealist' Forbes, Hawkins was also an early adopter of technology. He now studied his compositions on a thirty-two-inch monitor that lay not far from his spread of pre-potted paints and, from here, while dust accumulated on the drum kit, he planned larger works. There was still remarkable energy in his paintings, powerful enough even to overpower old Mrs McGillivary's wallpaper. This was mostly giant yellow flowers on a chocolate-brown ground with patches of green leaf. The painting looked great on Mrs McGillivary's wall, even unframed. A lesser work would have been swamped with foliage. As the walls of hunting lodges and town houses across the country found a solution to their bold wallpaper, Hawkins' studio expanded.

We all longed for public collections to buy work but, in Scotland, this had not happened since the Glasgow Gallery of Modern Art opened four years earlier. Public collections had closed their doors to all but a select few. We banged on their doors a few times with letters written to the Tate Gallery in London. You should invest in Helen Denerley's *Millennium Horse*, I suggested. Shirley Ann wrote to them too, but they added another lock onto the door with every letter suggesting that the establishment should look north. Even regional galleries took orders from above. I met the buyer for one of Scotland's public galleries at a client's house.

'I want a Shrigley, a David Shrigley,' she boasted. There was an *I'm Dead* sculpture available in Glasgow. In it a stuffed dog holds up a sign saying 'I'm Dead'.

'We're allowed to get one of them and they [the Tate]

will give us funds for it. Jack [Vettriano] is enraged that we won't take his work. He's offered it many times, begged us even. The more he does that, the harder I make it. We can't be seen to support commercial artists.'

'But Shrigley is commercial too, and so is Jeff Koons,' I reminded her. 'Very commercial.'

I liked David Shrigley's work. The cartoon-like drawings were always amusing, loose and free. But it was clear that a rift existed. 'Approved' artists always rejected craftsmanship and I found their work dull. The Tate Modern had opened a few months before, showcasing the Young British Artists. Damien Hirst and Tracey Emin were media darlings, the go-to heads for television. The previous year, Dundee Contemporary Art opened and I walked through its inaugural exhibition not realising that I should have pondered the sheets hanging from the rafters of every room. It is possible to take in a conceptual show like this at jogging pace and miss nothing. This is very different from Peter White's stony-textured heads which have a presence, a timeless face. Like standing next to a giant golden Buddha, no explanation is needed. 'Words are a distraction,' as he told me. It is the opposite with conceptual art. To enter this world, you must read the 'what the fuck is this' blurb and know the artist's name. Mostly it is only the name that is needed.

The last purchase from a public gallery since the

Glasgow Gallery of Modern Art was the year before. A Lotte Glob bowl was bought by the McManus Gallery in Dundee. Now, commercial galleries were alone. They had the Frieze Art Fair and we had others that popped up in every city. Kilmorack ignored all of them.

★

With every rule laid down, the freer Kilmorack became. 'No Art Fairs' let me focus on important things: artists and exhibitions. While other galleries joined the giant conga dance, Kilmorack fed its roots. Soon I was not content for the gallery to be a home for only Highland artists. I looked south and wanted more, much more than this.

Robert McAulay was the first non-Highland artist to show in Kilmorack. I'd visited him in his Glasgow studio the previous year. The tiny flat was his home before he moved on, so now it was devoted to painting. He kept the best of each series stored in racks high in the ceiling. McAulay had an air of dislocation. One half was in the here-and-now Glasgow and the other was elsewhere: as if he was born in one place but could sense another, better one in the glen just beyond; or maybe that love and hate were bound up in the same ball. He was a swan in an eagle's nest. McAulay's paintings had this feeling in them too. There was a tenement with its granite strength.

Looking out of a window was a face, and on ground level there were abandoned wellies, clandestine meetings and flowers that hid things. These are some of the sights seen and feelings felt by the younger, sensitive boy, wee Rab McAulay.

'I cannae help whit I dae. They just come oot, like it's nae me daeing it.'

His accent was strong Glaswegian and he was a dapper dresser.

'I'm daeing this set noo. I call them Rurals. Dae ya like them?'

There was a row of trees and maybe a house at the top of the painting, and a field that dripped in front. It was like a cross-section showing what lies beneath.

'Yes, Robert, I do.'

McAulay hired a van and drove up north with a set of paintings when he was able, and I flexed Kilmorack's fingers as far as they would go.

★

By the end of the season, only five miles away, another gallery had set up. Like Kilmorack, it was in an old church. There are many abandoned kirks in Scotland, especially in the Highlands, where the Church was like a hydra. The Church of Scotland's head was lopped off in 1843, to grow back next to a Free Church of Scotland head. This was lopped off too, and soon there were many churches in each town: Reformed, Associated and Free Presbyterian, next to the United Free kirk and the Free kirk. Next door to this was the Scottish Episcopal church, and, of course, there was the Church of Scotland and the Catholic churches too: and now new uses were needed for all these empty buildings. But a gallery in a church so close. It was a strange coincidence, and I knew its founder. I must have boasted again. I recalled a similar conversation to the one in Glasgow.

'I put things on the wall, people come and buy them, and that's all there is to it.'

How hard can it be? she must have thought, and, I know more people than young Tony. He's just a bit, you know. And he's rude to half the people that come in. It should be easy.

I should have warned her that running a gallery is not easy. It is more rarefied than most businesses and only the top ones survive. It is possible to open and never sell anything, before you give up and close. But imitation, I decided, is a form of flattery.

More Than This

2001/2002

By spring the following year a third church-gallery had opened up. This time it was only four miles away, in the old Free Kirk, which for many years was run as a soap factory. The soap king himself visited Kilmorack many times.

'I'm going to sell the old church and retire again. But, hey. Why would anyone want it? It honks like a bordello after all the perfume we've used, but you never know.'

In his tweeds he looked nothing like a soap king. This was a retirement business which had gone on for too many years.

I learned of the preview for the new gallery and planned to visit. The sign told me it was called 'Tigress Blue.' I heard the rhythmic thud of distant music the moment the Saab's door opened. Not long after this there was a soapy odour. I entered to a huge welcome.

'Tai-Chi-Dave! Welcome. Look everyone, it's Tai-Chi-Dave.'

Others greet the not-quite-me.

'Good to see you again, Tai-Chi-Dave.'

It didn't seem worth correcting, and so for two glasses of wine I was a locally famous martial arts master.

'This is the centrepiece of the gallery, Tai-Chi-Dave. It's a blue tigress that came to me in a dream, and it's taken weeks to paint. It will bring the gallery luck.'

On the floor there was a painting of a large blue tiger. This was one of the few marketing strategies that I hadn't considered.

'Goodbye,' I said. I tried to explain that I was not who they thought, but they had already moved on. Pizza had come out of the oven.

I may have looked like a martial arts master now – lean with distant eyes – but I was more aware of marketing than ever. I rejected art fairs, mostly because they're not fun, but I did like being in the Glasgow Art Fair catalogue, and I was not content to sit in a little pond, no matter how pleasant. I engaged the gallery's first outside help, from a design agency, and at the same time I booked a gallery to hire in a year's time in Cork Street. The designer's mission was to give Kilmorack a smart new look and to help put together a catalogue for the London show when it arrived. They would assist the gallery with all its design needs until that date.

The first thing a design agency does is attempt to figure out what look you want. I was a difficult client. They came up with all sorts of logos: circles with a dot in the middle, too breasty; accentuating the K, too Klansman; red, blue, yellow and green, too unsubtle. The grey, clean look of a gallery is the art world's version of a banker's suit. It is hard not to wear it, so we settled on a sans serif grey tone with lots of lower-case lettering. Sometimes, if we were feeling brave, taupe was allowed. This is the brown-grey colour of a French mole.

The first show of the year included work by Leonie Gibbs. The invite had gone to print before we imposed the gallery's greyed-down rules. It was a striped black, orange and turquoise flag with an image on each colour. I was shocked but it was very funky. I learned that three is a magic number. It works in many places: hanging, design and lists. Installation of Leonie Gibbs' sculpture was easy. The work was picked up from her house nearby and I was used to moving heavy sculpture from my foundry days. Her paintings, colourful and Matisse-like, were harder, because Leonie insisted on finishing her centerpiece, a Madonna and child, painted on a sheet of eight by four-foot plywood which now sits in a local church. It arrived on a tractor and trailer. Straw had stuck to the wet paint and embedded jewels had come off into the farmyard wagon. Leonie was not far behind. Her hair, a blond mane, made her taller still and, amazingly, her boiler suit added to her glamour. The secret is to tie a scarf around your waist, and roll your sleeves high enough to show bangles. She plucked straw out and glued back jewels, like a chef, and the dish was ready to be served.

'Voilà,' she said, and we headed to our homes to prepare for the preview. A few hours later and it began.

New clients always arrived. One, a director of an information technology company, bought a few large pieces of sculpture, including a life-size bronze of a lady rising from water. He was here to be healed by crystals and ley lines, and to make sure his chakras rotated and whooshed with new clarity. He talked of to alien abduction, dowsing in his high-tech company, and arranging the calendar around astrological transits. Maybe, behind our new digital world, lay older gods. They had followed us across its border and were under the surface of everything, lying hidden to most.

The traditional tweeded world still came, to shoot deer and birds, and hide in their castles. Some slowly declined. The man who had demanded that I played Bizet's 'Pearl Fishers' Duet' now demanded whisky too. He arrived in the glen driving a large Bentley, already drunk as he pulled up. The gallery was now a refuelling pitstop. Sometimes he would buy many works and eventually a cheque would arrive. And at other times he expected to not pay. I cut special quarter red dots to put under his purchases. The good also declined. Some inflated with gout and others shrank with age. This was only the gallery's fourth year and already, with such a large new clan, I was aware of each season and the changes that came with them.

The land slowly changed too. As autumn came, a headline appeared in the local press: 'Beauly Landfill Proposal'. It was proposed that all the waste from the Highland Region and much of Moray's old nappies, plastics and other waste too, should be dumped in the nearby quarry, making it the largest landfill in Scotland. They calculated that there would be four dump trucks a minute driving through Beauly and a deep queue of them waiting in the morning. They would seal the crap in with high fences and control the invasion of seagulls and rats with poison. We would need to get used to the smell, they said. Few people did not attend the village hall meeting that week. It was packed and angry. Eventually, the threat went, but there was a rip in what was once strong. The quarry had started small, to provide sand for the construction of the hydro dams in the 1950s, and as it grew it swallowed the past with each bite. Thirteen hut circles, two chambered cairns and a Pictish carved stone vanished. And we soon forgot they were ever there. Even the waterfall was dammed and gone from memory.

Thirteen years before this a lecturer in Edinburgh had told us fresh-faced undergraduates what he thought Geography and History were all about:

'Continuity and change is a great way of looking at

history. Some things remain unchanged over time. We all understand the motivations of Shakespeare's characters, while other things evolve or undergo catastrophic change overnight. To understand change, we must know the difference between these two things.'

The aging of clients was continuity: it is expected and will always happen; but the rip in the land was change. True artists are aware of this, of what is fragile and precious, and of what is a threat. No artist understood this more than Eduard Bersudsky.

*

After the three-hour trip to Glasgow, Tatyana sits me on a black fabric-covered box. She glides in small steps, her feet hidden beneath a tent-like dress. Her voice is syruped with Russian.

'I vill now svitch the lights off and begin the performance. I will geev you the full show. The works are old and fragile, so I do not do this often,' she tells me. 'Eet is rare. Enjoy.'

It is dark. A light comes on. With a rattle, the first machine comes to life. This is his self-portrait as an organ-grinder.

Bang.

A mechanical foot stamps a rhythm while a thin

metal arm slowly turns a mangle and a song begins. It is a slow Russian lament. Two eyes set within a face of burr and bison move from side to side and a mouth opens and closes. Below this, on a pendulum, rides a monkey, swinging on the organ-grinder's balls. Maybe it is the sad Russian voice in the background, or the stamp of the foot, or the slow fatality of the movement but I find tears in my eyes. This woodwose is the keeper of many dreams. One by one the machines tell the organ-grinder's stories. In the top-down world of Leningrad, where Bersudsky lived until he moved to Scotland in the 1990s, life was harsh. A nightmare about Stalin's purges is told, as well as the loss of a poet friend and the building of Babylonian towers. Rats are in control while all that is left is birth, sex and death. As one machine finishes, another lights up and I shuffle around the darkened room. Automata belong to the realm of dreams. They are the muted other that bring messages from places flesh can't go. There is nothing like this anywhere in the world and I have just seen the complete show alone in the dark.

The lights switch on and I return to the present. I am in a large windowless room with black screens, lights and the mechanical sculptures. Off this big room is Eduard's workshop and a kitchen. Bersudsky says nothing as he offers a cigarette. They are a long, strong brand. He picks up a bottle of vodka and gestures an offer of that too.

Tatyana explains. 'Eduard pretends that he does not speak English, but we all think he does. He just doesn't like words.'

Like my days of living in the gallery, socks, T-shirts and jeans hang from radiators. Other evidence of habitation is hidden from view in boxes. Eduard and Tatyana's life is not in Russia or Scotland, it is in this room, in the dream-machines that Eduard makes and the theatrical productions that Tatyana creates from them. I drive north with a few wooden carvings and a raven that swings its head and tolls a bell when a button is pressed.

'We use it as a doorbell,' Tatyana offers.

★

Back up north, the designers still worked on Kilmorack Gallery's new look. They made a fresh leaflet to replace the vile green one. The one with my own drawing at the top. The final folding sheet was simple, with the church's rafters disappearing into black on the cover and a spread of Leonie Gibbs' show in the centrefold. The art of good design, I learned, is to make many objects appear as one. A hidden grid helps, and you always subtract. You remove a colour so the white below is revealed, you get rid of a margin, a capital, a word. The more that is taken out, the stronger it becomes. It is easy to add but hard to subtract.

We began to work on the design of invitations and letterheads, and it was fun for once to work with others. I fed the designers images of artworks and they sliced elements away, refining. Large transparencies, negatives from 35mm cameras and digital images all fed in during this digitating time. It was only me that didn't change in this process. Baggy jumpers, shoulder-length hair, old shirts and a distant look remained. Maybe my skin thickened as I turned thirty-five.

★

Gerald 'the Pop Artist' Laing still came to all the gallery's previews. It was not for pleasure but to show support, and he took some joy in seeing it flourish. He was like a generous feudal lord who shines on some and avoids others when possible.

'I must put on a proper show of your work sometime, a solo exhibition,' I jested.

His profile was too large for any commercial gallery. Helicopters still landed outside his castle to discuss commissions. The last one I knew to land there was John Paul Getty's. It was a wildly silly suggestion.

'Tony, Tony, Tony. I'd love to. There's something about this space. The early work would look fantastic and so would the sculpture. Let's do it. Next August?'

That was it. A retrospective showing forty years of Gerald Laing's work would happen next August. This would include early Pop and conceptual art from the 1960s, abstract work from the 1970s and neoclassical sculpture from his newer periods. It was a coup.

★

Winter had become a different thing now the large stove was installed in the gallery. The cold blue note had gone, and water no longer froze overnight. There was always deep snow around Christmas, and the best sledging hill near Beauly was in the cow field by the cottage. There was often the whooping laugher of children as they catapulted down the slope. Cars parked the best they could and out of them came hats with bobbles, scarves and red noses. I had acquired an old green Land Rover which on occasion had to be dug out of the drive, before I headed to the village with a thick hat of snow on its roof. The winter preview was now special. The gallery was a place of light in midwinter, made warmer still by its pink walls which glowed out of the black as you drove past. At this latitude it is dark by three-thirty in the afternoon. Previews were now traditionally followed by a large pot of hot chilli in the cottage, where leftover wine was finished, chased with whisky. Helen Denerley never missed a preview. She was still the gallery's bully and I was her art-pimp. At night I listened to stories of wild Aberdeenshire parties and the gallery's progress was assessed.

'The new stove is quite good, and the kilt still works as a look for a preview. I can't believe I ironed your shirt for Glasgow Art Fair. The high roof space of Kilmorack inspires me. I will make some pieces that dangle. What, you don't like sculptures of geese flying up the wall? I'll make some of them too.'

Kirstie Cohen was always there too: consistent and steady. She always sold and her work developed gradually. The clock of an artist in oil paint is set by its slow drying time. Artists in acrylic have barely enough time to catch their breath before the painting is ready.

It was often two or three in the morning by the time I made it to bed, and I got up early to clear the debris from the gallery while guests slumbered in the cottage. The post-preview Saturday was a long one, but Fridays and Saturdays were celebrations. In Inverness, they always had been. Winter, now the stove was installed, was open.

*

What a strange dream to start the year with. There is a gathering at a hillside and we are pitching tents. Some people have magical powers and their tents fly in the air with thought alone, while the non-magical struggle. I am one of the magical, and I can feel others joining us. I recognise barely-known faces from the past, the magical ones, coming to this spot on the hillside, some more powerful than others. Little gestures give away their abilities as trains pull up to stations and boots tread paths to this spot. At one point a tall, thin man stands on a rock. His head starts rotating and a note comes from his mouth. It is a perfect note, a calling. What this means, I don't know, but I do feel good.

★

Running a gallery is like a long-distance train ride. The rhythm puts you to sleep and at the same time it stops you from slumbering too deeply, while outside the train's field-flashed window the landscape remains unchanged until suddenly it transforms. A viaduct high above a deep gorge is reached, or the sea. You awaken in a different place.

The May exhibition was like this. Lotte Glob's books sat on plinths, surrounded by Peter White's huge, geologically textured heads. There was also a flotilla of Lotte's floating stones arranged on the floor, and large story stones with poems written on them to sit on. Lotte was very relaxed about how it was arranged.

'I like the books standing up, and also when they're lying down. I'm happy with both, or if they're together like a library or stacked in a pile as if they are next to a bed. You set up the floating stones, Tony. Random is good. It's interesting to see what someone else does with them, so you do it.'

Peter White was more specific.

'The triptych will go at the end. The largest head will go next to the curved desk, and I would like the small paintings to be in a cluster. Let's not have any interpretation. Just let people decide for themselves.'

The triptych opened and closed like Hieronymus Bosch's *Garden of Earthly Delights*. In Bosch's painting, the centre panel is the garden and the right-hand panel is a hellscape. When closed, Bosch's triptych shows the world in creation, and its five-hundred-year-old riddle still riddles today. Peter White's triptych was just as mysterious. On it there were two heads, one with eyes closed and the other with eyes open. 'Eyes open' held the other's head in a healing position, and on both foreheads were scraps of paper, tied on with string. On each side-panel were the remnants of vases. When closed, it became a book, and you had the option of hooking it shut when the urge took. I joked with Peter that some things are life-affirming and that his paintings were death-affirming. He didn't laugh but nodded in agreement. There was more than this, but he wouldn't tell me what. Lotte Glob's books had secrets too, written on ceramic pages and sealed closed in the kiln.

The gallery was transformed in this exhibition. As the church exuded its stony presence, the metaphorical train reached a point, and on day two, sometime in mid-afternoon, when the sky darkened and Fauré's *Requiem* played loudly, it was as if the old church had been created for this one service. It was dark and saturated inside the gallery and paintings, sculpture, kirk and light joined in a Damascene moment. A client was in the gallery and we looked at each other and said nothing. Silence is a word. Peter White was right; it is hard to explain.

★

It was during this show that the Russian artist arrived. She entered carrying a small child in her arms and looked intensely at everything, dissecting the gallery into colours and forms.

'Yes, I'll have a coffee. No milk. Have you got brown sugar instead? I am staying not far, outside Kirkhill, but we plan to buy something in the area. It is good to see a gallery here. I am an artist.'

The way she used the words implied power. I learned that she was from Moscow and had lived in London for the last ten years. The galleries she had exhibited in were some of the best. Her eyes scrutinised me and I plumped my feathers. Her eyes stripped you bare, like naughty X-ray specs. She left, and a week later bought the old schoolhouse, a mile from the gallery.

★

By August, the train was approaching its biggest transformation yet, Gerald Laing's retrospective exhibition. The oldest work to be shown was from 1963 and it was almost four metres high, showing the actress Anna Karina in black and white dots. Gerald invented the dot painting at the same time as Roy Lichtenstein. A large green canvas from this period, *Lincoln Convertible,* was also included. This was painted as a response to President Kennedy's assassination and it showed his head falling forward in the boat-like car. They were painted almost forty years earlier and the canvases had a different quality; they moved like old but solid sails. There were paintings and prints of skydivers and astronauts, when Gerald caught the speed and excitement of his time in America: cars, thrills and girls. Another early work was the *Hybrid* project. It consisted of a small leather suitcase, little bits of fabric and lots of data.

'Tony, Tony, Tony. You know this was quite significant at the time,' Gerald told me as he clicked open the case.

'We were really taking the piss, trying to find a work of art that would suit every person in every house. It was a joke on the uselessness of numbers. I can't even remember what the result was. The ultimate artwork was a small orange-coloured corduroy painting of a landscape, I think.'

The heaviest work was his *Hamburg Triptych*, which consisted of three iron panels that represented Gerald's time spent in Germany. It was a dark period for him, and four of us were needed to manoeuvre it into the gallery. The parallel tracks left from the wheels of the lifting trolley still show on the gallery's floor today. During a tea break, a large wooden crate was delivered. Gerald liked tea in mid-morning and would drink the scalding brew down in one, eager to continue work. The box was the first professionally packed museum crate I had seen. It had been sent by his New York gallery. Screws were exactly an inch apart, and thick ribs reinforced the box's already sturdy wood. Inside, in two white vacuum-packed halves, like the yolk of an egg, lay a small chrome blade.

'Oh that!'

Gerald picked it up and threw it in the back of his open-topped Austin Seven. He didn't care much for his mid-1960s abstract sculpture. By the early 1970s Gerald was fabricating monumental work from Corten steel. He had moved to the Highlands and these works were a celebration of the rugged landscape. There was also a phallic energy in the upward-pointing pyramids. We could send seeds back up to the stars, they suggested. There were many bronzes included: some from his earliest, most abstract period, which was almost Cubist. As the years passed, Gerald's sculpture included more features. First hair and then eyes. By the 1980s his sculpture included portraits and relief panels (like the *Hamburg Triptych*) and now, Gerald explored movement and myth. The most recent work was the maquette for a new mercat cross to go into the centre of Inverness, and it had some of Gerald's recent favourite things on it: unicorns and sundials. Scotland, he told me, has a surprisingly long history of the sundial for a country with so little sun, including a portable version. The manual for this, to help find the correct latitude, he informed me, is less compact.

Spread out in front of me, Gerald Laing's work seemed incredible. His Pop Art contemporaries from the 1960s never moved far from their roots, and they became establishment figures: but Laing could not help chasing passions.

'Tony, Tony, Tony, I can't help it. They kicked me out of the club when I left New York. I could do anything when I was there, and they'd think it was wonderful. It was a kinda hell. So I left and became apostate, cast out. Well fuck them. It's good to be alive. Last year, I sat next to Paolozzi on a plane. Two old sculptors: it was coincidence.

He said, "My best work is done, Gerald. How about you?" I thought and replied, "No no, far from it. There's a lot ahead."

And that was true. He had started to paint again. This was an exhibition that should have been shown in a national gallery. Sometimes it's good to be apostate. Better apostate and interesting, than establishment and boring, I had learned from Gerald.

He spent three or four days visiting the gallery and turning his ear to conversations. He waved people on meekly and observed their movements around his work. This was one reason for putting on this exhibition. Despite his castle and the elite worlds he had moved in, Gerald wanted more. He wanted to be loved by the people.

*

New folk always arrived. There were men with waders rolled down their bodies, or with socks that went up to their knees. One lady had so much money in her handbag that I followed her around picking up the fifty-pound notes that fell out. I returned them. 'Whoops,' she thanked, and crammed them back into her bag. It was a trusting atmosphere. The greatest test was when I drove to Durness that autumn and accidentally left the doors open all day. Leaving at seven-thirty in the morning, I returned in the evening to find 'thank you' notes and money on the desk. There must have been quite a few quiet wanderers around the darkened gallery that day, delighted to have the place to themselves.

Life was good. If it was sunny, I sat on the new patio at home catching the last of the evening sun, and if it was cold the cottage was now warm with a new stove that didn't smoke. The gallery was a rewarding place to be, but I wanted something more, more than this. The words of Black Allan drifted back. 'I can see you here with flowers in the garden, a beautiful lady and maybe a dog.'

The flowers were there. Neck-high delphiniums and lupins were at the side of the cottage, catmint at the front and buddleias, bushes and copper beech planted elsewhere. He was right. I needed a dog. The next morning, I drove to Elgin with a friend to view Chloe, a springer spaniel puppy.

'She's a wild one. Not bad, but crazy. You'll have to keep her outside in a kennel. I've found her impossible to walk.' Chloe's owner holds up a short thin lead, more suited to a cat.

'You walk her on a lead?'

'All the time.'

The three of us drove back: my friend, Chloe and I.

'You can't call her Chloe. It's a crap name for a dog,' my friend suggested.

'I agree. It has to be an artistic name: related to the Scottish art world and it should end in a vowel. How about Peploe?'

'Peploe it is.' My friend removed the small cat collar. 'Here's to freedom.'

'Bonjour Peploe,' I said.

The Hug

2003/2004

'You do it like this.'

She embraces me closely. I feel her body: its heat and heartbeat, and I squeeze back.

'No, no. You've broken it too quickly. There's no point hugging if you push the person away at the end.'

I was being instructed on how to hug by Shona Leitch the ceramic artist. She made sensual porcelain vessels that curled organically like a body. Occasionally Shona worked in the gallery. I repeated the hug and held it for longer.

'That's better. Your homework is to practice with Peploe.'

Shona's mission was to address thirty-six years of untouchability. In Scotland, a handshake is intimate, so is a barely noticeable head-nod. The double kiss of France or Italy is completely alien and even a hug is a quick thing: a squeeze followed by a push. Shona told me to be more open, to let the love flow. This was easy with Peploe. It is almost impossible not to cuddle a spaniel puppy, even if you are Scottish. The puppy was wild to begin with. She ran endlessly around the one large room in my cottage at night, until I tied her to the leg of the coffee table. After this she learned to lie down and to watch and listen for instructions. As if the dog was part of Shona's school of hugs, Peploe continued my training and pushed her head against my lap when the word 'cuddle' was said.

A dog's primary concern is to look after the pack. They are gatekeepers that open the door for some with a tail wag and the offer of their soft fur, while for others they slam it shut with a snarl. A dog also ranges ahead of you, readying the ground before you arrive. 'Make way, for my great master is approaching,' is a dog's silent message. It could have been the buoyancy of the economy, or maybe it was Peploe and her secret commonwealth of dogs that cleared the path and brought joy, but in this tiny corner of the world metaphoric flowers were everywhere. People were optimistic and united, or perhaps it was just me.

Peploe and I visited Michael 'the surrealist' Forbes. His work was now more sinister, but it was fun, the macabre joke: a cat with a machine gun, birds sitting on a crocodile's head surrounded by feathers with the title *Where's Bob?* Michael Forbes was happy in his painting but worried about the rising water of the river near his house. His daughter was besotted with Peploe and soon there was a springer spaniel in their home too. The same thing happened with the Russian artist. We visited her in her homely family kitchen. There was an Aga, food, dishes, drying clothes and children's drawings. Peploe added to this intimate scene and a few weeks later she too had a spaniel puppy. Our visit was to arrange a show of new work and she agreed to create fresco boards (plaster-covered panels) with loose nude studies painted on them. She studied icon painting in Russia, and these fresco boards would use some of these traditional elements, even tempera using egg yolk mixed with pigments. As we were about to leave, she lowered her head and looked at me with puppy eyes.

'Will you do me a favour? I am in a terrible fix and I need someone to babysit tonight. Could you look after the two boys? Please, please, please.'

So that night I played with Lego and then sent the boys to bed while the Russian partied. Many local people were helping the her out. Some babysat, others changed plugs, loaned lawnmowers, or built websites. Round here, in the Highlands, people help when they can.

Allan had moved from delivering bad local wines to becoming the darling of the local art groups. They loved the poetry of his stormy seas, skies and mountains, and his sure-footed confidence. He was a man who knew where he was going, and his next trip was to the isolated archipelago of St Kilda, a helicopter ride from the north of Skye. He planned to paint an entire exhibition to show the following year from this visit. 'I'm still surprised you're here. Incredible really. And you'll do a catalogue too for the St Kilda paintings? Great, I'll call by when I return.' We had a plan. This would be the main August exhibition for 2004.

Helen Denerley had a dog too. She always had one and now it was Molly, an aging lurcher, an alpha female. The dog sat on a bed of sculpture packed into her Isuzu Trooper car. The time had come for Helen's first solo show in Kilmorack. Over the last few months, I had sat at my computer arranging pictures of the last five years of sculpture. They'd been given to me in photographs, slides, transparencies and now digital images too. It is easy to create a fine catalogue if pictures include a life-sized Indian bull, an eagle mounted on a large mountain boulder, a fabulous scrap horse, deer, dogs, a camel, the wolf pack and a fourteen-foot-long lizard made from oil drums.

Helen liked to do things big. The previous year she and American sculptor George Beasley built a symbolic bridge across the Deskry Burn at the bottom of her croft. It was made from molten iron poured into a mould at midnight. The party around this grew so large that night that hamburger vans arrived to feed the revellers, and a satellite link with a university in America was set up. Helen's dog Molly guarded her home while Peploe ran wildly through the guests. They avoided each other.

'Why Hare, Moon and Sky Hawk?' I asked as we freed the sacred cow from its cage on Helen's adapted trailer, untying blue rope from the ploughshares that formed its vast buttocks. 'Oh, no reason other than it sounded good. Animals have always been sacred, in all parts of the world. I wanted to get the feeling of deep wonder and importance.' No one pointed out that there was no such bird as a 'sky hawk' when the catalogue and invitation arrived on their doorsteps. The phone was already ringing with interest.

Sculpture unloaded, we hung the show, or placed work around the gallery. The sacred cow, or more accurately well-hung bull, dominated the centre. Its belly was made from a copper water tank and the float inside it ticked like a heartbeat if touched. Around this, an ecology of sculpture evolved. Birds were high up on wires; wary hares made from mudguards and hammers listened from the distant end of the gallery and dogs looked you in the eye as you entered. Spotlights were turned from the walls into the centre: a rebellious act in an art gallery.

At the post-show party, Helen's dog Molly guarded her car and Peploe sat at my feet near the large bonfire. They were kept apart.

Helen Denerley had more animals than most. In addition to Molly the dog, she had Scarface-Scratch-the-cat, horses, chickens, ducks, and all the wild creatures that surround an Aberdeen hill croft. Even when snow-trapped during the long Aberdeenshire winters, there was a clan of sorts around her.

Gerald Laing had his Jack Russell, Phoebus, and his son, who now ran the foundry, had a younger Jack Russell, Vulcan. For a short time – because large dogs are only with us for a short time – Gerald had deerhounds too, Asgard and Odin. Large hunting dogs to go with his castle. Eventually, he changed from using mythical names and acquired a little white dog he called Patch. Leonie Gibbs had so many dogs it was hard to count them. They hung around her kitchen sofas like a band of thieves, monitoring who entered their den with one eye open. James Hawkins opted for two fine huskies. The only artist not to favour dogs was Suzanne Gyseman, painter of fairies and mythical creatures. She was surrounded by cats, insects and a rat. Sculptor Illona Morrice loved vegetables and at one point also kept a rat. Everything grew in her garden.

Let the love flow, Shona my hug-trainer instructed, but in many ways an art dealer is always surrounded by love, for art is an intoxicating torrent of goodness. Paintings and sculpture come from a quiet communion with the universe. As I planned exhibitions, Allan MacDonald sat quietly looking at the Atlantic that surrounds St Kilda; Helen Denerley worked from her croft and was part of its animal fabric; Gerald Laing rediscovered his Pop Art roots, using them to make the world better; Peter White meditated in his cell-like studio and the Russian artist painted her kitchen and family. The machine behind great art is love; and deeper still is the love of the hidden mathematics of composition. A painting can pivot around the smallest red dot, the slightest sound in a sea of quiet. It is not the mathematics of numbers but of instinct.

★

The unveiling of Gerald Laing's mercat cross was that summer, and I found myself on Gerald's side of the plush red rope. There were kilts and tartan trousers on this side of the line. Prince Andrew appeared in a brief cloud of his darkly suited people and then vanished unmissed. Gerald waved, and a convoy of guests headed to his castle for lunch in a large marquee. It was like a wedding, with pre-set seating and a three-course meal: soup, venison and pudding. I was placed between a long-time journalist friend of Gerald's, who smoked roll-ups as we ate, and on the other side, a thin man in a suit, one of the property developers behind the new shopping centre who commissioned the mercat cross. I discover that sometimes commissioned art is not about love. There was only one purpose for the mercat cross, and that was to redefine the heart of Inverness. The old cross was a short walk away on the High Street, and Gerald's cross was now the centrepiece of a freshly built square in front of a new shopping centre. He saw it as a place where lovers could sit kissing on its steps, while the suited man next to me intended for the huge mercat cross to spin the map, and with this, take people to his new temple of commerce. Gerald's friend next to me smoked and drank red wine. She had lived everywhere and seen most things. She already knew that big money often had an agenda, so this wasn't news to her. It was part of a game of rich man's chess. Eventually, lovers did sit on the steps of the new mercat cross as Gerald hoped, and people visited the latest shopping centre too. It did move the town's centre as the suited man planned. The next time I walked past it a bus was parked there. On its side was the logo for Channel 4's latest reality show, *Big Brother*. A lady popped out, blocking my path.

'You must have an interview and appear on our next series. You'd be great. I can see that. Can I persuade you?'

'No.'

That wouldn't have happened next to the small, rain-worn mercat cross that people now walked past without noticing. Gerald did far fewer public commissions after this. He had seen both sides and chose the people.

Leonie and Joe Gibbs were at the unveiling lunch too. Leonie glided through the white tables with wine glass in hand. There were rumours of a music festival. This was Joe's project, using the hidden sunken garden explored by me and Black Allan seven years ago as a rock stage. Joe jested in a new accent: now with a hint of Californian hipster.

'Yeah. Tone. We're going to make it groovy. We'll call it Tartan Heart and it will be small and beautiful. There will be love hearts everywhere and tepees. It'll be beautiful,

Tone. Yeah.'

*

It was not long before their festival happened and I walked the sunny field, moving from one group to another, like Gulliver, but instead of Yahoos and Lilliputians, it was peopled with faces from the past and present. Some were from the bars of Inverness and others from the streets of Beauly. A few more were from half-remembered parties elsewhere. These were lives I had forgotten when I walked through the church's door, reinventing myself as an art dealer, and it was good to be reminded. James Hawkins and Helen Denerley were at the dance tent, Hawkins setting up a light show. Michael 'the surrealist' Forbes had his own tepee. He'd swapped a painting for this wigwam and had set it up earlier in the week. Allan MacDonald was there briefly. He said it was nice but a little noisy for the locals, which included his parents. Kirstie Cohen and her gang were there, and Illona Morrice too.

Throughout the festival were clients I had met over the last seven years of art dealing. Even Gerald Laing turned up briefly. It was a local thing but soon, like so much, it grew. Fences went up and security guards were shipped in. Some of them were not used to the dark trees and hooting owls at the furthest festival gate.

We called Allan MacDonald's exhibition 'A Northern Land', and in it MacDonald went beyond the role of creator of paintings into that of the brave explorer. The catalogue showed him perched on a cliff or grasping trees – and the paintings were elsewhere paintings, messages from windswept places told through a paintbrush. This 'dispatches from remote places' way of working had become the core of MacDonald's art. It was northern romanticism where, instead of forty days and forty nights in a desert, a Scottish artist seeks enlightenment in wetter places. There were three characters in MacDonald's St Kilda paintings: the moving mass of the Atlantic, the dark wave-battled rocks, and the light that is occasionally glimpsed. This light was subtle, mostly obscured by cloud or a rocky mass. It was elusive.

'They're fantastic Allan, but a wee bit gloomy,' I suggested.

'A gloomy effect, maybe, but somehow the opposite happens, don't you think? These pictures lift our spirits and glow with excitement.'

He was quoting from a review by writer Michel Faber and was pretty happy about it. It was unusual to see MacDonald without his splattered romper suit and old walking boots on. Today, the preview, he had a trendy shirt. He had been to the same shop as me. It was the quick way to show that you had made an effort. Soon we were not alone. The gallery heaved with bodies. It was like the sea in MacDonald's paintings and, like St Kilda's islands, the painted land masses of his work rose above an ocean of heads. There was a brief argument outside before we opened the doors, a scuffle over who would buy *First View, St Kilda* and, now opened, there was the viral spread of dots all art dealers dream of. Gerald Laing appeared. 'Tony, Tony, Tony, I was wrong. So many people, again. It's just as busy as the first opening. It's incredible.' I looked around and happy faces were everywhere: the scruffy, the kilted and the now slightly tipsy. We were a sea moving together.

*

'Now, let me see how you've done,' Shona Leitch the ceramic artist has called by and unfurls her arms for a hug. I hold her body close to mine and I am now better at it. I don't push her away but keep holding. I count to ten seconds as she instructed. 'That's good. That's very good.'

Dog Food Days 1

The picture painted so far is incomplete. Rather than a gradual ascendance, a gallery's life is far more of a roller-coaster ride. Like bees gathering nectar, a little should be kept aside for winter, but this is never easy to do. When sales are slow and the money stops coming, the façade must remain, while underneath it becomes ugly.

'I can submit these accounts, but you run the risk of them asking how you survive,' the accountant said.

I survived by never being rich. I took no holidays and did vast amounts of specialised work myself. With good practical skills, the cottage and the old church building could be kept standing with little more than a ladder and a bag of nails – and the swan would appear as bright as ever. I had learned to be self-sufficient. Electricity use in the cottage, for example, was only £4 a month – the cost of boiling a kettle in the morning and a dim bulb at night. In the Highlands new clothes counted for little. Here a well-made, faded old shirt was as high-status as a new one, and ancient cars were fun and could be coaxed into life for years with old Ian the mechanic's help. A trough, I learned, would always rise to become a crest again, and then I would purchase a well-made shirt.

Gallery finance was always seasonal. In June rich fishermen arrived and purchased medium-sized landscapes that took my bank account onto the good side again. Sales dipped in July as families passed through, and then in August big buyers often bought large pieces that fattened the bear before winter. Winter was survival only, waiting for the Easter rush, and hoping that not too much extra cash would need to be pumped into the gallery from my credit card. One show would often do incredibly well, only to be followed by an exhibition that should have done better. It was not worth thinking 'if only,' because it was too unpredictable to make a jinx-wish. I learned to trust the future: that if I wanted company, it would walk into my life, and when money was needed a sale would come, and it did . . . eventually, if you could last that long.

Others, especially those with young families, found it harder to weather the dog food years. When the money dried up, their partners complained. Some were sent to teach by their wives, others saw stacks of paintings piling up and became disheartened and others, once stylish peacocks, began to wear tracksuit bottoms and not leave home.

'I'm sorry Tony, but I have no money to frame them or even to buy canvases.' The worry spots on his face had grown over the last few months and his movements were different. They had become erratic and directionless. He was worried about keeping the car on the road. 'I'm lucky the wife is working but I'm stuck here with the kids. It's a bit of a downer. Any sales would be appreciated.' I left praying that I'd sell one of his works soon. An artist needs to paint to remain healthy and the gallery must keep going too. There are few greater moments than handing an artist a large cheque, and there are few greater disappointments than handing them a very small one. I just kept going.

London
2005

Winter had been far longer and deeper than expected and there was snow all the way from Inverness to London, even in late February when Kilmorack's Cork Street show was planned. I had rented a studio apartment overlooking Piccadilly Circus, and exhaust-spewing vehicles formed an endless river of noise. Above the cars, buses and taxis, large neon signs advertised oversized corporations. I had squeezed my fat feet into thin black shoes and they were already soaked through from the short walk to Cork Street along the slushy pavement. Next to me was James Hawkins' wife Flick. She was helping for the week: a bit of polish to my scruff. She was responsible for logistics, which she did with ruthless efficiency. She had arranged for a lorry to collect work, which included Helen Denerley's Sacred Cow sculpture and bronzes by both Leonie Gibbs and Illona Morrice, as well as some of Lotte Glob's books, a large Peter White triptych, a vast truck full of other paintings and a few cases of wine. Flick had found the studio apartment too and she pondered as we walked.

'Corkscrew! I knew something was missing. It should

be the first thing packed. I'll drop my stuff off and then head off to get one. No, I'll get two in case one breaks.'

The gallery looked wonderful. It was the first time I had hung an exhibition on white walls. In Kilmorack, the pink was dramatic but unforgiving. The reflected light cast a pink sheen on everything, which made it harder to see all the colours in a painting, and shadowy corners turned pitch black in Kilmorack. The white space was completely different. It was airy and light. Flick dropped her bags off and disappeared into the grey streets.

The art-filled lorry had pulled into Cork Street around lunchtime the previous day, and work piled into the rented space. There were four of us: James Hawkins, Flick, Helen Denerley and me. Soon we were joined by James McCallum, whose loosely painted figures were included in the show. He had discovered that it is easier to support a family by working on film sets than it is as an artist and that was what had brought him to London. He spent half the time here and the rest working from his studio outside Fort William.

It is an assumption that artists are solo creatures, concerned only with themselves. This is not always the case. We were a team: Hawkins measuring to centralise the huge Peter White triptych and Helen Denerley arranging a corner with the work of the more allegorical artists: Forbes, Scott and Kate Leiper. I was trying to get the credit card machine to work and Flick made sure there were no slackers. We were joined by the Russian artist too, towards the end of the hang. She arrived eating a late lunch and sat on the desk, a tear in her left eye. 'But this is terrible. You have put my work towards the back. It's not good enough. I would like it here, and here, and here.' She indicated the three main walls of the gallery. A second tear followed the first, and a third when I said 'No.' She pushed a swell of anger upwards.

Hawkins took control. Maybe he knew this game from somewhere in his past. He handed over the spirit level and measuring tape to me and sat on the desk laughing with her while we worked, and when her lunch was finished, he guided her round the gallery and out of the door. 'Do you mind if I bring the boys to the preview tonight?'

'Yes. Definitely no kids allowed at the preview,' Flick replied, and the Russian artist left.

★

When my grandfather worked in London from the 1950s until the '70s, Cork Street was the place for a gallery to be. It buzzed with energy. The Pop Artists, St Ives group, old masters: all the best artists were shown at packed cutting-edge previews, where wine was passed around by pretty waitresses and large ashtrays filled with butts. Now it felt like almost any other London Street and these shows were only memories.

Long thin gallery spaces were on the left of the road, some behind closed doors, and Waddington's large gallery sat on the other side. Cork Street felt increasingly forgotten as more galleries moved to other locations or, in some cases, now only attended art fairs. As the weather flashed between snow and sleet and a curtain of rain fell from the gutter in front of the gallery, it seemed unlikely anyone would arrive to see our northern offerings.

'Wine anyone?' Flick suggested, and the huddle of artists and I stood and looked out onto the wet February street. The first guests arrived and hung their dripping coats in the little kitchen. Slowly, one by one, the room filled and the one wet coat grew into a soggy mountain. There was the rhubarb-chatter of a polite cocktail party. At first there was only the occasional sale, not the rash of red dots hoped for. A week earlier, a stream of visitors had made their way to the almost snowbound Kilmorack Gallery. They had come to see and buy from the amassed work that awaited delivery to London. This was different.

The biggest excitement of the night came from a Chinese man in a black suit and mohair overcoat. He wandered the white space with glass in hand telling us about the work on the walls and eventually he came to his conclusion.

'I'll have that one [Peter White's big triptych] and those [Denerley's two dogs] and those [Gibbs' bronze heads,] and those two large paintings. I'd like them too.'

His list grew so big I asked him to slow down. Some he wanted reframed and others reserved for longer. He left his business card and promised to return tomorrow to finalise the deal. We discussed him over dinner.

'He's a fantasist,' I suggested. 'Of course I know Ian Scott's paintings, he said. A guy in London wouldn't be more familiar with his work than any other artist in the show. Ian Scott is mostly New York, Wick and Edinburgh. He was faking knowledge.'

Helen Denerley suggested a real buyer would never follow red wine with white wine. 'That's an alcoholic, not the head of a powerful company.'

'His shoes. They were worn. You can always tell by the shoes,' Flick suggested.

'He was smiling and moving his arms too much. Real buyers are normally more composed,' I added. In a gallery, a reserve must have an end-time, when the red dot will be removed if a deposit isn't paid. We agreed to leave it until lunchtime the next day, and in the morning we would phone the last gallery to hire this space. That was the previous week and it was Edinburgh's Scottish Gallery.

In a hired gallery you adjust labels, play games on your laptop and wait. If a new Bentley pulls up outside, you check your fly and tuck in your shirt, while the limousine's occupants get out and then saunter in the wrong direction. You cannot leave. Occasionally someone comes in. London visitors are different from northern clients. One man, or was it woman, was in full drag. He sat on the desk and told us with his strong London accent how today he was feeding his soul. There were girls selling flowers and artists looking for a gallery to show their work in. At one point a Russian property magnate entered, with his tiny, traditionally black-dressed mother, wife and two immaculate children. He too was feeding his soul. Years later, like other oligarchs, he was accused of theft.

It was time to phone the Scottish Gallery, and I asked to speak with Guy, the grandson of my spaniel's namesake Peploe.

'You were here in London last week. I'm just wondering if you were visited by a Chinese man and if he showed interest in lots of work. Too much work and too good to be true. We've had this guy in and something seems a bit dodgy.'

'Ah. The Chinaman. Yes, he wanted lots of stuff and we sent a few works for reframing. I must stop them. We're still waiting for money. He's a con.'

He was a fantasist. Cork Street had frequent openings, and if he wanted a glass of wine and some fun, he would remove his now sagging and dirty chief-executive costume from his wardrobe and become what he really wanted for a night: rich, powerful and part of the often closed world of art. There was, of course, still lots of free wine at Cork Street previews.

Some things he couldn't disguise. The pristine fingernails of the rich man are hard for a working person to fake, and so too is the look of a man who has houses in many countries, but no home. I like to think that some of the dirt on our fantasist friend's mohair coat was cat hair, and that after his weekly adventures in Cork Street he rolled home to a friend.

*

My London adventure ended and we packed up the lorry. It headed north and like zombies Flick and I caught a tube to Heathrow. Glasgow Art Fair was hard work and this was the same. We limped homeward exhausted. I waved to a client in the airport. He was reading the Bible while waiting for the plane. Six months later, when he came to Kilmorack again, he commented 'You looked terrible. What had you been doing?'

'Just art, just showing art. It's not so easy in London,' I replied.

Whomping

2005–2008

Every stone was frozen when I finally made it home to Mill Cottage. In the gloom of its dark interior Peploe wagged her tail. 'Bonjour,' I said. She had been returned by a dog-sitting friend who had tried, but failed, to light the fire, so I lit both: the solid fuel cooker and the wood burner. It would take days for the heat to reach the icy corners of the cottage, so I retired to bed with a double duvet and, on top of this, I put a sleeping bag.

It was March 6th, and still as cold as midwinter. Warm sun can arrive at any moment and when it does, the transformation is quick. Second duvets and jumpers are taken off and hidden at the back of wardrobes. Thermals are removed, skins shedding so that life can return to the naked bodies underneath. It was, I decided, a good day for a thinking walk. There is something about the rhythm of a walk that clears vision and I needed to digest London and the previous seven years of art dealing. I felt change in the air. The twelve-mile Loch Affric walk was perfect for this.

★

It is only half an hour's drive from the gallery. I am already booted, so I head quickly past the birch and Scots pines to the start of the walk. My feet are heavy on the dirt road to Affric Lodge, which sits perched on its island looking down the loch, and I am impatient to get further, to a place where my feet will lighten, and spring me from stone to stone. There is a skeletal tree where last year an eagle landed close enough to hear the flexing of its orange feathers. This is the forty-minute point. I stop my whomping rate at a stream and stand to listen. There is the sound of water, birds and wind on all sides of me. I am immersed.

As I whomp along the path, a leaping walk, London falls away. The thin black shoes don't fit, I think. Fantasists, oligarchs, Fortnum & Mason corkscrews. Crowded airports, black guys in blue boilersuits and white guys in grey suits. Seven years a dealer. Black Allan. Mrs MacRae. Thoughts bound through me. It's harder now, than it was, to sell paintings. But I do.

Peploe is ahead of me. She is enjoying this rapid pace. I throw a stone deep into the heather and she brings it back. The ground is still frozen underfoot. The evolving world. Not just me. Computers, phones, images. Land, money, generations. I am making rapid progress along the path and I don't slow down when I reach the river but leap across the partially submerged stepping-stones, moving so quickly my boots don't get wet. It is at this point, an hour into a thinking walk, when thoughts slow down and clear. I made a monster to feed. We all have. There are London monsters, art fair monsters, monstrous mega-company monsters. We are all like monkeys, too afraid to let go of their branch and leap to a better one. How to rein in my monster, the Kilmorack beast? I must be happy to fly through the air, knowing that a branch is there to grab. Different times. There's no model to follow. I plan, I build, and a course is set. To my right is Sgùrr na Lapaich. I am small in this landscape, very small, but here, like the golden eagle. I am held upright by the confidence of each leap from stone to stone. It is good to be invisible – but now seen, I should do what I like. Why am I still here, while others aren't?

Thoughts flash back to my childhood. I am five years old, dressed in wellies and duffle coat with my mother's wartime Brownie box camera around my neck. It is a Sunday walk outside Edinburgh. I am on a stone wall at the edge of a field and a horse comes close to the camera. I look down into the camera's upward-facing viewfinder and click the silver button. When the 120 film is developed, there is a ghostly horse and a flare of light filling the black and white photograph. After this I had a cheap soviet-made camera and, when old enough, I studied magazines and acquired a Pentax SLR. Cameras

had always been part of my life. I am still moving swiftly. The path is nearing the end of the loch and to the
left is boggy cotton-grass. I am fifteen years old and the
youngest person at the photography club. I have shadowed
my father because I understand photography as well as he
does. He has just put a darkroom into a cupboard, and I
am developing a film: chemicals capturing light laid down
when the shutter was pressed. I whomp on and realise that
I was the only kid who did these things. It is part of me,
the camera, and now, in the digital age, it would become
vital again.

The rhythmic bang of feet is shamanic: whomp,
whomp, whomp. My mind skips to artists. Once Highland
artists, only. Seven years ago. Quality, quality, quality. I must
reach out to southern artists once again. There are many
more, worthy of Kilmorack. I have a list in my head. Find
a contact, make it happen. I am now at the westernmost
point of the track, one and a half hours into the thinking
walk. This is the point where symphonies are composed,
novels written and cloudy skies cleared.

I walk quickly on and ponder changes: impossible
changes, unthinkable. I flash back. I am seventeen and it
is the ten-minute tea break in St Andrews Woollen Mill.
The air is uncuttably thick with the fug of fifteen women
chain-smoking in the small room. Ten years later and in
the bars of Inverness, tobacco tins sit on the tables. That

has gone. They have been replaced by phones, and now, a pint too is gone, before you drive home. Cars are bigger. Trucks are bigger. Roads are fatter. The richer are richer. Holidays and toys for all. We have so much. I whomp past someone. It's the man from the tyre centre, and we nod to each other in recognition. Digital. Everything is digital and big. The gallery's first web-sale was three years ago, a Kirstie Cohen to Spain, and now others come in on occasion. Digital images, digital print, emails. London was real, but ignored, the wrong crossroads to strike a deal. The virtual continent is now populated, but art is physical, the ultimate tangible. Images, design, communication. Some towers are tumbling and some rising. It is a race to flatter with invitations, catalogues, branding. Everyone needs the confidence to leap from branch to branch, letting go of one to get further. I can build confidence with design and artists, and let the world decide. And the world, the digital continent, has no geography, no London.

The track on the other side of the loch is wider. It feels as if the walk is ending, now there are no rocks to bound from. The rate is steady and fast. I have a plan. The 'Highland artist' label is too geographic for me now. Quality is far more thrilling, and I want to be thrilled. That is what pumps the blood. A focus on Scottish artists is good, for now, in an international context. I enjoy and understand photography, and I'll develop these skills so there is a record of all works. Seven years ago, with film and transparencies, this was not possible, but now it is. I have the design skills too; and the slick sans serif gallery style is already there. It is about confidence. I don't need London or art fairs, just vision. Our feet are barely touching the ground by the time Peploe and I reach the car park. The short drive homeward is tree-lined with swooping corners. It is warmer and the frost has gone, so the second duvet and my white thick-ribbed jumper are put to the back of the wardrobe. It is spring and the new gallery season opens.

★

The first exhibition of 2005 was already an exclusively non-Highland show. After London, the big truck headed south to Devon to fetch Heather Jansch's driftwood horses. Like Helen Denerley, Jansch repurposed material, reincarnating driftwood. Wood, being organic, gave her sculpture the galloping muscularity of a horse. I had seen these incredible sculptures in the London Art Fair in Islington a few years earlier, and it was hard to forget them. McAulay was also showing again. Abandoned cookers and cars, trees, shadowy people, texture and composition were the subjects of these paintings. The third artist was Nael Hanna, pronounced 'Nile' like the river. He had left his native Iraq on an art scholarship and had never returned home. Hanna's oils had the creamy fluidity of a breaking wave. It is good to show three artists. The gothic geometry of the old church rewards mathematics. It is strange, but three is a good number. Just after this exhibition Jansch's work went viral. Images of her horses photographed on a Devon beach were circulating widely on the early web and almost instantly there was a three-year waiting list for her sculpture and a new price tag that reflected this. Photography, I thought. The power of the image.

An exhibition is many things. It can be a group of works shown together in a room, but it is really a gathering of works. They are held out to be seen. The roots of the word are ex, out and habere, hold. Next, I planned to show how many artists started work with a drawing. This is where they are often most free. Some play with a line. Under a James Hawkins painting, with its bold and bright acrylic colours, lay a very different beast, an almost Japanese minimal line. Lotte Glob's etchings took her away from the technicality and restrictions of clay and into the underbelly of her work: the hidden communities a child's eyes see in rocks and sea. Her scratchily drawn marks windowed this world, and hinted at her European roots too. Peter White's drawings were very different. He pushed hard, sometimes with so much pressure that the paper was ripped into its underlayer. Michael 'the surrealist' Forbes's ideas sat naked on the page without the dressing of paint. The Russian artist, of course, had brilliant drawings. This would be an exhibition that showed, held out, the personality of a drawing. An offering, a chance to learn. That is one of the joys, the thrills of a gallery.

Come summer, there was shock news. The quarry that six years earlier almost became Scotland's largest dump was under threat again. This time plans were for it to become home to Scotland's biggest electrical substation, and from this serpent's head, a body of pylons three times as large as standard pylons would snake down Scotland's spine to the cities of the south, devouring trees and wild places in its path. Behind this was a drive to repurpose the empty spaces of the north and make lots of money while doing so. Politicians had always visited the gallery, not canvassing, but because they had taken time away from Westminster to walk in the hills. Earlier still, after the Second World War, hills were a place for recuperation. Socialist walkers headed north from Glasgow and the government encouraged access. Mountains were sacred and in Scotland we were proud of them. Something had changed.

Booted and Gore-tex-clad politicians no longer visited the gallery. They holidayed elsewhere and were replaced with wind farm prospectors, who enticed landowners with secret lucrative offers that were hard to refuse. An estate that was once a money-losing vanity could, with wind farms on it, earn its value every year. And the wind farm company could earn even more.

I flashed back to student days. The eighteen-year-old Tony, skinny and scruffy, was active in the Green Party. On our first stall, the manifesto was for the 'Ecology Party', but our name had just changed to the Green Party. Long-haired vegetarian girls visited our stand. Opposite us was the Young Conservatives' stall. In the late 80s, young Tories took pride in their outrageous behaviour. Posh, fat boys with red faces and a beer in their hand visited their stall. The green movement was growing, and I arranged a speaker to talk every week. One debate was 'commercialise and become mainstream' versus 'be spiritual and offer a purer vision'. It reflected the debate in the rebranded Green Party.

'You need to be in power if you are to change things, and it's what we all want, for green ideas to become mainstream,' suggested Dan. He was a wiry kid with a flat cap and had just jumped ship from the Scottish Student Socialist party. 'But, man, what's the point if you become your enemy,' replied Tosh. He had a round face with a huge nose and ears poking out of long greasy hair. Now, many years later, it seems Tosh was proved right. The green movement was used as greenwash, forgetting its small-is-beautiful ecological roots. A few years later a visitor came into the gallery. She was young and I was single. We got talking. 'What do you do in Wales?' I asked. 'I work for a public relations company. There's eight of us in the room. It's quite secret. Our job is to make it so that every time someone sees an image of a wind farm, they think of positive things: lambs leaping, blue skies, nature, a better future. We slip images of wind farms in whenever we can. That's our job.' She looked mildly embarrassed. The church building, that day, hosted a confessional.

The giant electrical substation, pylons and wind farms that threatened the glen would be a difficult battle to win. Goliath had grown even bigger. Change was definitely in the air.

Looking Within, and Out

2006–2008

A church building is inward looking. You need to look upwards first if you are to see out. The direction I look is towards fresh artists and technology. Reinvention is vital to a gallery, but its speed is set by the slow heartbeat of exhibitions. Even a weekly visitor should see something new every time they come in. It is a space that fidgets. I planned a new catalogue: one that an art collector could not ignore. I started with a number: 1.618. This is the golden ratio, which I was surrounded by in the church's arches and alcoves. Mathematics had buried itself deeply into the church's architecture. The difficulty in hanging an exhibition, or designing a catalogue, is being neither too empty nor two crowded, and for this I could look around me, to the walls and roof, to get inspiration. Layout is instinctive, but, I hoped, guided by this geometry, so I built the golden ratio into the new catalogue. On the front was Helen Denerley's camel in the snow with the gallery's iron-gate door open behind it. The photograph was high contrast, like night-time lit by moon on snow, and in a new non-standard size, the golden ratio a secret hidden inside its body. This was a technical toy that was fun to play with. There was always some disappointment when a box of new catalogues arrived, but this one held together well and now I distributed them with more confidence.

Finding new artists was a slower process. First, you must become hooked by a painting or sculpture and it should pull you back repeatedly. It is a form of love. Seeing Henry Fraser's freely painted character portraits was one of these moments. His work was simple, mostly a head and shoulders painted with big, bold brushstrokes, but there was so much soul in each small eye that I could not walk away. There is a code that makes it unthinkable for one gallery to ask another gallery for an address. You must seek them out, Sherlock Holmes fashion. To find Henry Fraser I recognised the frames, and then the framer. From here I knew he was within six miles of central Edinburgh. Two years later, I found Henry's number by phoning every Fraser in the Edinburgh telephone directory. 'Hello, are you Henry the artist Fraser?' I asked. Eventually, after many calls, a 'yes' came back and I drove south. This process took several years.

By the time I met Henry he had become a success. He was a few years older than me and I was surprised because of his sudden appearance on the Scottish art scene. 'I thought you'd be younger,' I said.

'Aye, lots of people say that. I guess I just found my feet

a little later than some.' These feet were bare, and his face had large features and dreadlocks. He heated up vegetable soup and tea and I was reminded of Snow White's dwarfs. This was a friendly house and Henry Fraser was at home in it.

'You know. I've discovered that it's OK to enjoy what you're doing. The best work doesn't need to come out of a bad place. It can be win-win. There's no real need to suffer for your art. That bit's a myth.'

'And your inspiration? Where do these paintings come from?'

'I just start painting and something emerges. Maybe it's someone I've seen from this window. I've spent a long time in this room, looking at the world out there. Things and feelings come, eventually.'

Paintings leaned against each other on the floor or were on the wall for consideration. Some were barely started, and others are almost finished, just waiting for a final mark. A few waited unresolved for years. I left Henry and his large auditorium of faces and packed a few new works carefully into my old Saab before heading north.

★

Finding Hock-Aun Teh started with detective work and ended with magic. His work was familiar to me from the Gallery of Modern Art in Glasgow and from art fairs in London. The paintings were large and abstract with vibrating reds, life-giving yellows and intense blues, blacks and purples, and created with incredible energy: paint explodes onto Hock-Aun's canvases with giant controlled marks. Hock-Aun himself is a mystery. He was born in Malaysia and studied art in Glasgow and now flits between the two, or to China where he has fans. He also founded the martial art Tukido and is called Master Teh by many. He is clearly not your average Scottish artist.

There were only four Tehs in the phone directory, and I discovered an address near Glasgow with a phone number that didn't work. I wrote a letter but no reply came back. It seemed Hock-Aun worked behind the push-button coded door of a large network of studios near the city centre, so that is what I would try next. It was November and the gallery was closed for two weeks after eight full months' trading. I woke early. Today is the day to find Hock-Aun, I thought. I was on the train by eight and in Glasgow by eleven. I had no phone number, no appointment and no plan. The hunter's instinct was switched on. An art collector collects art and a gallery collects artists. This is madness, I thought, as I walked the streets towards his studio, past cafés and shop signs with incorrect punctuation. I was no longer at ease on grey pavements or surrounded by tall stone buildings. I don't even know what he looks like, I thought, but on the final right turn onto his studio's street, halfway down, there was a man who could be him.

There was paint on his shoes and he wore a once-blue boiler suit which now creaked with thick paint where brushes had been wiped, and ricocheted colours, bounced from canvases, had left a galaxy of dots. He was short with black hair, stylish glasses and movements that were more like teleportation than a walk. This could be no other person.

'Hock-Aun? You must be Hock-Aun Teh?'

'Ah, you must be Tonee. I have been expecting you. What do you know about chi? Please come up to the studio.'

Being in the company of Hock-Aun was like dropping a pill. From here time sped up. He showed no sign of surprise at the unscheduled meeting. We bounded up three flights of stairs. The studio was long and high with a line of windows on two sides and large canvases stacked so deeply they took up a third of the room's width. One wall, the only clear space in the chaos, was where he painted and viewed work.

'Tonee, you must look at this one: *Catching Rain in the Gobi Desert*. Good, isn't it.'

He threw the large canvas onto a small bent nail and told me how he walked across the Gobi Desert without water, and how, when he finally met a group of nomads after ten days, it seemed like a crowd, a mini-city. This painting was whisked away and left to balance precariously next to him and another, *Hunting Wild Boar with an Englishman*, was put onto the bent nail. When in Malaysia he hunted boar, not with guns but with hands and sticks. The Englishman was another art dealer and he found it terrifying, Hock-Aun laughed. More paintings flew onto the wall, the discards left balancing end to end like a game of spillikins. We dashed to another stack of canvases and all my limbs were used to help extract *The New Year Feast Ends up with a Game of Mah-Jong*. Large yellow marks suggested the movement of people.

'I try and capture energy, the chi of a moment. Not the things. The energy of heavy rain in the jungle and a fire at night. My work is about energy.'

I touched a mark in a canvas. It was an indent, deep enough to leave a bump at the back.

'Yes, sometimes I make a hole with the brush and go right through. Ha ha.'

Hock-Aun was a man who showed no fear. He told me how he smuggled himself into Iraq via Afghanistan to see the overthrow of Saddam Hussein and of vast one-man exhibitions and commissions in China, and he never stopped moving while he spoke. Slowly to the window, a quick turn, and back to the easel in a leap. This rubbed off on me, and I too moved like this for a while.

★

The search for new artists kept the gallery fluid and fiery. They are the magma that stops a gallery's stable of artists setting solid, but the walls of Kilmorack could only take two or three new artists a year. Exhibitions go watery if there are too many artists and, with too little new blood, they lack the elixir of new life. It was surprisingly difficult to find thrilling new work, despite, on some days, receiving as many as four requests to show in the gallery. Some were ridiculous: the mother who came in with her four-year-old daughter's drawings rolled up inside a Barbie doll tube. Some were sad: abstract explorations of the cancer that had killed their mother. And some were mad: collaged letters encompassing quickly-emitted paintings, and photographs overwritten with red-painted words. I dismiss these.

A gallery is judged by its last exhibition and the rogues' gallery it shows, and there was little space for whims. Most requests to show fell into the awkward middle ground: neither bad nor exciting. They were too much like something else. Sometimes it was the artist's technique that set the direction, when heart and soul needed to come first. Rejection is the hardest part of running a gallery. There is no easy way to do this. There is always a question. When will it be less full? Should I do landscapes? More weird? But the ship must sail on and leave them in the water, toughening my skin further as it goes. Don't look back, I thought, or I will join them. It is I who seeks the artists.

★

Ronnie Rae greeted me with a hug. It was like being enveloped in a mountain. He had been carving stone for forty years and his hands were like sledgehammers.

'I'll not keep going for long, Tony. Granite is not like other stone. It is unyielding. It fights back. Ma hands and ma back. Soup?'

We had homemade lentil soup in his studio above Loch Lomond. 'Ronnie is a genius,' said his wife Pauline.

'Acht no. I have a compulsion, that's all.' He swatted away the compliment and his voice filled the kitchen. Ronnie did more than carve life-size animals from stone – granite. He did delicate things: burning designs into dried leaves, weaving his drawings over newspapers, painting, poetry, refashioning old suitcases as art. He was a spring of creativity but he was massive, like the mountain the spring flows from. Soup was part of his life: frugal living, vegetarianism and maybe, sometimes, a little whisky. He told me how he visits the National Gallery in Edinburgh and walks past every painting until he reaches the Rembrandt self-portrait. When there, he stares at it for half an hour and leaves. I took some smaller pieces to show the following year; granite sculpture is too heavy to be moved easily. When I looked in the rear mirror, Rae stood waving, looking like Moses with his full beard, and Pauline, much smaller, next to him.

The 2006 gallery catalogue included a black and white photograph of a life-sized wounded elephant carved from granite. The mass of stone and the weight and fragility of the elephant on its knees was powerful. It sold to a prominent figure the moment the catalogue arrived on his doorstep, and the sculpture was helicoptered into position in the buyer's sculpture garden in the south of England. He bought directly from Ronnie, bypassing the gallery, but this kept Ronnie and Pauline in soup for years . . . they were nearly out. I never told them where the sale came from.

I wrote a letter to Steven Campbell too, and he died just after I sent it, aged fifty-four, before I could visit him. It was the scale and psychedelic vibe that drew me to his work. Another letter was written to neoclassical sculptor Alexander 'Sandy' Stoddart, and I visited Sandy the following year in Paisley. We met in his studio, a clay and plaster-filled temple to the neoclassical world.

Scaffolding was set up to work on a large sculpture of eighteenth-century Scottish scientist James Clerk Maxwell. On a table was a model of Ossian, to be carved into a hillside somewhere in Scotland. Sandy saw that I was not a neoclassicist like himself. My eyes showed no recognition at the more obscure Greek and Roman myths he mentioned, but Sandy was swept by the current of neo-Platonic certainty, and into a world of harmony and beauty. Outside this world were ugliness and brutishness. He asked me which artists the gallery showed and he shook his head disapprovingly. They were too brutish.

'And Gerald Laing? He loves the classical world,' I tried to win Sandy over, but Gerald had also been part of the Pop Art movement and had sinned because of this.

'Where does Picasso fit into art? The dabbles of a primitive. We are trying to show beauty and life. Picasso goes the other way. He is a brute, going backwards.' Gerald Laing sometimes held similar views. Before the gallery, when working in his foundry, I heard an artist asking him for his thoughts on his own work, a bronze portrait just cast in the foundry. 'It is easy to make a monster,' Gerald had replied, and walked away. I told Sandy that I could see what Picasso saw in African work: power comes from the material, people, magic, local gods.

'Then Tony, you are a philistine too, a child who has not moved on.' That was the beginning of the journey, I am told, and we have come so far: Greeks, Romans and Egyptians. Sandy's role was that of the scholar, Socrates, and I was the pupil learning truths understood long ago when planets orbited the Earth in perfect spheres. He removed his sculptor's coat – it was white with an old-fashioned collar; the type Rodin would have worn – and we drove in convoy to Sandy's house.

We drove through Paisley, past poverty and multi-generational substance abuse, and into a leafy Georgian cul-de-sac. Paisley has been surprisingly important to Scottish art. Many prominent artists came from this small town: John Byrne, Marj Bond, Jock McFadyen, Ian Cook and others. When I was a child my two elder brothers, twins, had paisley-patterned pyjamas. Mine were sky blue and I was jealous. I loved the paisley pattern. It was exotic and beautiful.

Sandy Stoddart's house was a side of Paisley I didn't know existed. Outside, it was the sort of grand stone home you see across much of Scotland – two bay windows and stone steps up to the front door – but inside showed the results of a fastidious classical mind: beauty. The paint used on walls was clearly applied as lime washes and distempers, the colour the pink of the gallery and curtains thick and long. Sculpture was everywhere, and books and the odd wine bottle. In the hall was Stoddart's *Pimlico Priapus*, a rectangular depiction of the famous priapic god, but missing his well-known phallus. 'The London council wouldn't allow it,' Sandy said, reaching into a drawer full of penises and attaching one to the sculpture, 'but here he can be the god he was meant to be.'

★

On the other side of the country, in Aberdeen, I found Joyce W. Cairns. She was buried deep in her studio. Outside, there was a biting easterly wind. It was the same November wind that chilled my St Andrews youth, and there was a familiar masochistic comfort in it. It was the wind that blew across the school playing field. The breeze across Stoddart's Paisley was much softer. It was cold and damp inside Cairns' studio, but the old gospel hall she worked from was large enough to accommodate the wall-sized works racked along two sides of the room, with stacks of bubble-wrapped paintings on the other two walls, encircling a warm, heated core. This was the nucleus where she sifted through family memories and collected observations of Footdee, pronounced fit-tee, the fishing village that squats around Aberdeen harbour just beyond the door. A towering oil supply ship heading out into the North Sea dwarfed the small cottages of Footdee as it passed. Aberdeen is a hardworking city and the world pulses through its oily, nautical arteries. Joyce Cairns was like this too, and, like the city, had sometimes been overlooked by Edinburgh and Glasgow. She made two mugs of coffee and looked proudly on her achievements.

'I like to work on a hard, smooth surface. Why would anyone paint on something that bounces or is rough? I want to be in control. You know, there's a lot that goes into one of my paintings this size. I'll not do many more.'

Much of Cairns' work was on a grand scale: a complex web of figures and remembered objects that jigsawed together to riddle the viewer. They were every bit as good as the work of celebrated men further south. Most paintings were too big to remove from the racks, so we headed to her house for warmth and lunch. Her home was narrow like all the Footdee houses but taller than most of them and inside, unlike her studio, it was immaculate, with white-painted, steep staircases and the work of other artists on the walls.

'It's time to leave Fit-tee. When the house has sold, that's it, we move south, closer to civilisation. But I've loved Fit-tee and the art school. Sometimes it's time to change.'

'You're brave,' I suggested. 'Your work will change. Footdee is special.' Maybe the biting easterly wind was behind the move, or a desire to see the other side. Aberdeen artists were a tough, dedicated breed. It is the last stop before the north. I too would dream of duck-down duvets and fresh linen sheets if I lived in Aberdeen. I left with a few small paintings for the Christmas exhibition and drove west, home to the river, trees and gallery.

★

It is like climbing a mountain. One small step follows another, incrementally gaining height. Looking forward there are peat and rocks ahead. That is my world. But when you look back, the car is a dot, and then the car park, until eventually everything that is not in the clouds has vanished. I leaped from one catalogue to the next: the night-camel cover, to a dappled door, and in 2008 the booklet was textured, with an embossed silver logo. Incrementally upwards from exhibition to exhibition: a sell-out iconostas show by the Russian artist, a return of Allan 'the landscape' MacDonald and an exploration of 'Art and the Word'. Upwards until the world is left behind. The old kirk was covered in scaffolding and the lime harling repaired, etching the harler's hands with acidic lime in the process of its re-shelling. I found a manufacturer of gallery lights in Scotland and slowly re-illuminated the gallery professionally.

As I leaped, the world leaped too, changing, engorging and digitising. There was a new brand of client that occasionally contacted the gallery. In 2007 I was phoned and told to expect a visitor. Later that day seven black cars pulled up. Security looked around and then a Russian oligarch entered, followed by his leopard-patterned besilvered wife and English-educated young son. At the back, as with other oligarchs, was his black-clad mother. His private jet was stranded in Inverness awaiting a part. Where he went, so did an entourage – and an entourage, limousines and security, could be summoned at short notice if you had the resources, even in Inverness. He was interested in two small paintings and wanted a fifty per cent discount. I answered with disapproving eyes. It was not his fault. He was disconnected. By dinner time the oligarch, his family and the two small paintings were in Moscow. Within a few years he was dead, an open verdict.

Outside the gallery, there were still plans for Scotland's biggest electrical substation with its tail of giant pylons. Massive timber lorries now rattled the gallery's windows as they passed, taking trees to be pulped or burned for biomass fuel. One of these stopped to let another large truck coming the other way pass, and I noticed that the timber lorry was almost as large as the old kirk, built to awe people with its size. Something was bigger still: invisible and increasingly omnipotent. Slowly it surrounded us, a layer of hidden information and wealth-creating algorithms. Unseen, it influenced the powerful – politicians, journalists and businesspeople – changing the world. In 2007, with the launch of the iPhone, it entered all our lives. I looked down after my climb and the world was transformed. The old church with its fresh yellow harling and new lights hadn't looked as good for a hundred years. And the people? They were on their phones.

PART IV

Value

The Silent Spring

2020

I awake early and splash water onto my face. My beard is full, with a white goatee in front, and my hair, Jesus-style, is below my shoulders. My nose is larger and my eyebrows have bushed up. I tell Globbie the spaniel to stay and guard the cottage, and she wanders in and out of the open door until Kapka awakes to make a strong morning coffee. We have changed together over the last ten years: Kapka rediscovering nature, and me, I shed my youth, and have become a man. Love opens doors too. I use the electric bike – a practical vehicle to take me to a magical place. I still get a thrill opening the old church's double doors. The paint that was flaking off twenty-five years ago has been rubbed away by wind, rain and shoulder. The crows are gone now but there is the hollow drumming of a wood-pecker not far away. I open the door and enter. I know I will not be disturbed, for these are unusual times. The only visitors are delivery vans.

Since the bank crash of 2008, I have built display screens large enough to sit with the size of the old church and not look small. They have wrought iron ends and a heavy, hand-built feel. I slide one to the edge of the gallery. Today I will video Ian Westacott and Raymond Arnolds' two-person etchings and then photograph the newly arrived Mark Edwards White Wood works. Elsewhere in the gallery there are comfortable old chairs and wooden chests which I have picked up in auctions over the years, and there is technology everywhere: twin monitors, computers, iPads, a streamer, softboxes and polarising flashes, even a 3-D camera. I am well suited to this nerd-embracing high-tech world. The coffee machine whirrs as it grinds the beans. They still deliver freshly roasted coffee beans from Inverness, even in plague days. I like to work barefoot when no one is around, and I play Toots and the Maytals at high volume. It has never been so busy, in a virtual way. I set to work.

I place the Canon D5 on its gyroscopic tripod and film a floating shot of the gallery and the current Westacott-Arnold exhibition. It's not been a good time for 'exhibitions', and this group of prints is important but has not been seen. Westacott and Arnold have worked together when possible for twenty years, making two etched plates of the same subject that are combined to make one print. Westacott and Arnold are an unlikely duo. Ian is large and gentle with a mop of once-spectacular curly hair. He has lived in Scotland for thirty years and never lost his laid-back Australian drawl. Tasmanian Raymond Arnold is small, quick-moving and dressed with flamboyant confidence. He was ill after his flight to Scotland and we thought he might be the Highlands' first case. Today he prematurely heads back to Australia, over fire and plague before he is stranded here. There are too many reflections from the glass on my floating video so I abandon it. Westacott and Arnold are the real world: ink, paper, trees and a twenty-hour-flight-time friendship. There are no ones-and-zeros, nothing digital, just a shared space and the scratching of knife on copperplate to recreate a memory, a dreamtime. Maybe that floating space is now everywhere, woven digitally into our lives.

Behind the gallery there is a cloud of long-legged hovering craneflies that have made a home in the hedge planted to separate the kirk from the graveyard. It is not a large space, but I have left it wild and untidy to help the beasts. Last year a young deer used it as sanctuary while its mother went off each day before returning to her offspring in the evening. The hedge is alive with small birds flying in and out, and there is the scurry of small voles underfoot.

I move on to photographing Mark Edwards' *White Wood* paintings instead. He has painted this series for many years. There is always a Homburg-hatted man standing in a snowy wood. Sometimes a train, a building, or more hatted men are seen. Each painting is like a chapter and this year, of all years, there is a fire burning amongst the trees.

I picked these works up a few days earlier, driving the eerily empty roads north in my large red van, to his studio in Tongue.

'Hey Tony Baloney,' he greeted me sounding like Coppola's Godfather. He was a jester one moment – 'There's nothing in these paintings, just something I do,' – and then he was serious. 'I have to keep the story evolving. It's not what you see in them, but what is outside it, just out of frame.'

'And the burning?' I asked.

'It's just what happened. How the story evolved.'

Edwards was one of the city-fleeing freedom-seekers from the 1960s who ended up on the north coast. Lotte Glob was another and Gypsy Sall too. Edwards and his wife raised three kids in a remote cottage with no electricity and now he was older and the kids gone, Edwards entered his white woods world. There were always warm colours visible just below the white snowy surface, and a deep texture that the painted chapter is woven into. I left Edwards in the old shop he used for a studio. It was hard to drag him out of this painted snowy world.

I photograph these paintings and put them on the website before emailing out to clients. They are sold by lunchtime: some to America and others south to England. There is no geography in this floating world. The only customer who still visits in person is Jim the retired banker. After all these years Jim is still ninety and he visits every week, buys a painting and drinks a coffee. 'How do you keep so young?' I ask.

'Oh, I enjoy everything. I awake grateful, don't eat too much and I'm not scared of what is coming. Not at all.'

'Living is not the same as not dying.' I surprise myself with my reply. Everyone is thinking strange thoughts these days. Jim leaves with another small landscape tucked into his blazer.

Outside the gallery the harling needs repair. It is eight years since it was last done: streaks of grey now run down the once perfect yellow exterior and there are bare patches where, in the winter, ice has expanded and popped out bits of lime which I pick up and place in a small pile. Time has passed.

The electric bike's motor sings as I cycle to the cottage. Walking would be almost as fast but my body is used to moving quickly: to rushing from one project to the next. There's jus du jour waiting – cucumber, lime and apple. Kapka is performing her morning Qigong routine and Globbie sits attentively at her feet. It is ten years since I first saw her at the side of the road picking berries. 'Do you dance?' she'd asked.

'No, I have two left feet, but I can pick a few brambles with you.'

The cottage now has rugs, candles, a bathroom full

of potions and more books on the shelves. Gone is the clothes-drying string strung across the kitchen.

★

The autumn of 2008 seems like another lifetime. Nothing and everything changed then, with the financial crisis and the banking bailout. Show still followed show, but the tumbling interest rates and the removal of fat-cat bonuses sliced away many traditional art buyers. The gallery's upward-pointing sales graph halted and began to head downwards. Outside the gallery a giant anti-pylon banner hung. We fought an impossible battle. There was a public debate in Inverness and on the stage, on a single chair to the right, sat the Highland Council's lawyer. He wore an old tweed jacket, a regular shirt and his everyday trousers. On the left of the stage was a two-tiered platform and here sat Scottish and Southern's lawyers dressed in greys suits, white shirts, ties and some with open laptops. The odds were stacked against us. I had already spoken with our round-faced, well-dined politicians. The Liberals' MP told me it was already signed and 'in the bag', and the Scottish National Party politician was irritated by anyone who wasn't with him. He didn't care. People and nature are an inconvenience when you are important and sit at the board table. An elderly Conservative politician told me he liked my car, a blue Triumph Stag from 1971. Soon the pylons and substations were built, and the protest banners repurposed as tarpaulins to keep log piles dry. Pylon wires are not small. They are large and heavy, and cut the sky like a fence divides a field.

★

It is noisy with birds in the garden and there are more of them than ever: the most recent refugees displaced by the ever-expanding quarry. When excavation began, badgers and deer passed through the garden too. They were starving and looking for a home. Two weeks earlier, when everyone was told to stay at home, they sent lumberjacks in to fell the Caledonian pine, oak and birch trees so the big diggers could move in. Within days of felling, the trees were pulped. We sit outside on the patio, Kapka, Globbie and I, with sun on our faces, surrounded by a whirl of birds and a mist of craneflies. It is a very loud silent spring. I set off back to the gallery on the electric bike.

Mitigating Measures

Henry Fraser has sent five new paintings. He has found it difficult to paint over the last few years. There are too many people around his new, very social, studio. He now rents the old one in his house to a lodger. Henry saw injustice whenever he switched on his iPad – Scottish independence, plague and poverty – and painting seemed an indulgence amid these frenetic distractions. I told him that it is needed, it is part of the cure, and eventually these new works slow-bussed up to the gallery. I photographed them, added them to the gallery's website, emailed out and they were sold by dinnertime.

It wasn't this easy in 2008. We all struggled. When sales dropped, I bought a Giclée printer and created a separate print website. Bring art to the masses, I thought, in desperation. Eleven years earlier I said 'start at the top and work down', and this was my first down. Giclée printers are large and ugly. They swallow expensive inks and paper. It sat upstairs, square-pegged within the roundness I had made, and the chug-chug printing noises drove me crazy. The gallery was already a monster and it had now swallowed another one. Some work looks good as a Giclée print. It can reduce its size, clean it up and make it into a nice thing to hang in the kitchen, but it is not real. Oil paint is particularly hard to photograph, especially the thick impasto of Allan MacDonald and the dark skies of Kirstie Cohen. Every reflection shows in the photograph, and sometimes an artist instinctively works with the shadow created by their brushwork. Subtle areas are difficult to capture too. An off-white that blends to cream on the canvas can show as only off-white. Even using the finest papers and on the most expensive Giclée printer, the magic is lost. There is no shadow, less colour, no history. It is not real. Buying a print is not cheap either, once it is framed. It is wiser to buy a small painting instead.

After six weeks the Kilmorack monster spat out its little intruder. The printer was gone and the world was quiet again. It had not been a wasted experience. I knew that down isn't a direction to travel, so I looked to London again, and research began on photographing paintings, cross polarisation and colour correction software.

I found my direction again. In the fog of 2008 I had dropped my compass. A gallery is a synapse, I was reminded. It allows artistic neurons to flow between artist and client. We must encourage this transmission, the impulsive spark, and so I headed back to London. A powerful club had invited Kilmorack to exhibit there. Maybe it was the top of the pyramid that needed to be fed, so in 2011 I accepted. At night the streets of Belgravia are quiet, or maybe it's just that the grey suits and quiet black cars disappear into the shadows unseen. We rattle small suitcases towards the club where we will stay, echoing in the empty street. There are no signs suggesting this is the right place, only a flag and a brass plaque with a number. I ring the bell and we are ushered in and scrutinized. In this world members wear suits and ties, and the staff scuttle in shirtsleeves, rising from the basement when needed. The chairman is notified that we are here, and he welcomes us with the look of a disappointed father.

'The lady is perfect, but this is not good, or this or this.' His hand waves around my curtained-hair, stubble, mismatched trousers and jacket, and old tie. 'But we can make an exception for a few days.' We head to our room, up an elevator and along a corridor, chuckling at a 'member resting' sign as we pass. And then we explore. Kilmorack has been invited to hang work in the large sitting room where comfortable sofas are placed next to tables where china teacups can rest. Here, deals are made, before they go to parliament or the boardroom. If something is 'in the bag', it has been bagged in a room like this. We have dinner in the club too, in its vast nineteenth-century dining room, which is upstairs past rams' heads and royalty. It is just us and another group that are dining tonight. There are two menus for the same meal. A ladies' menu without prices and the gentlemen's with them on it. The chairman is right, it is not a good fit. I am a scarecrow in a suit that can't even fool the crows. I recall a nightmare I had forgotten, in which I return to student halls of residence to start a new life and wander from room to room, older and not fitting into the past, before I wake in a sweat. Our fellow diners are discussing club business. Someone is being given a last chance before being blackballed, and current changes are being assessed. Someone in the group has a eureka moment and raises his voice. 'There's nothing left to do. We must go back to the old ways.' Everyone agrees, they liked the old ways better and that is the new plan, to bring back the old plan.

Six months later and we hang the old-fashioned sitting room with work, mostly landscapes but there is sculpture too: Gerald Laing in the dining room and Helen Denerley's snarling scrap-metal hunting dogs in the small garden. There are other events in the club at the same time – a ceremonial meeting with gowns and regalia and some very drunk Canadian ladies visiting the UK. They mistake me for a chef and congratulate me on some finely cooked pork. My sister visits a few days later because she is passing through London. In the sitting room when she enters, men change from speaking in English to Arabic and draw the chairs closer. By the time our exhibition ends and is packed up into my red van, the doorman is relaxed and friendly. He is short, stocky and kilted, and fond of his strange nest and the weird birds that visit it. It is a long drive north. London, I remind myself for the final time, is not for me.

★

Sales gradually recovered after 2008, but it was slow. This time I was waiting, scanning the horizons for what I wanted. This time it was new ways of controlling information. As a gallery grows so does its data, and I had moved from three spreadsheets: sales, clients and inventory, onto to a homemade database. It was a raggle-taggle affair. The old string and bits of tape solution. It functioned but only just. The website was the same. It was like an old jumper that you put back on and realise is full of holes and is stretched down to your knees. I looked out and waited for technology to catch up. Technology is nothing special, just a way to solve a problem.

★

I move through the gallery like a wizard behind an emerald curtain, with a staff of hidden software helpers. One database now replaces three and it is created specifically for galleries, keeping its figures in a cloud that never clears. Kilmorack was one of the first to sign up and now the provider has grown to be an international company with many staff and multiple offices. New work is updated to the website automatically and it slowly evolves when the outside world changes. Photo software is no longer pirated. It is expensive but works on all computers, which synchronise automatically. There are three identical workstations: the garden, the eagle's nest and the sales desk – which makes my flow of work so simple. It is the swan's trick that keeps it smooth above water. I am connected to the real-but-yet-unreal virtual world. I must become Prospero mastering an island with spells.

★

After the crash of 2008 galleries tried other things. Many offered interest-free credit for buying paintings and we became form-filling question-asking licenced credit brokers. It was always strained: my client stands before the gallery's desk. He is wearing a white, teasingly transparent onesie and wishes to buy a bronze. He clutches his hands together when excited and strikes a balletic pose when thinking. I go through the stipulated questions. How much do you earn? Dependants, children? I'm not happy to ask these. They tumble down the role-played fantasies which people create in a gallery. The form is then signed in three places and in triplicate. He has no children but would have loved it if he had.

It was a scheme designed to encourage a new type of client, younger, to buy paintings like a sofa on hire purchase, but most people that used it were the very wealthy, who just enjoyed playing the financial game.

His Range Rover is parked outside and he is in front of the desk, his trousers tucked into his long socks. 'Interest-free credit? Banks don't do that very often. I would be a fool to not take it, but, of course, Tony, I don't need it.'

They smiled when it came to the 'how much do you earn' question and ticked the top box.

Eventually I sent a customer copy to the bank rather than a bank copy, and this choked the well-planned system of the large bank that backed the scheme. I like to think that is why this supporting bank suddenly refused to work with galleries – me sending the wrong form. It took a year to be paid while they charged fees and the costs of having a credit licence. Nowadays I suggest something informal, no questions asked. I know most clients anyway.

The greatest mitigation measure is to keep hunting for artists, to be the best.

★

I drove to the centre of Fife to visit Charles MacQueen and his partner Christine Woodside.

I parked the black Saab next to a high wall. There was only one entrance, a large grey door set into stone, and no sign or number to show that this was the right place. It was opened with a long guillotine lever and I entered a dense garden whose paths had been swallowed by green efful-gence, so I pushed through, making my way to the house. There were, I discovered, several paths, but they didn't lead from the grey gate to the house, instead taking you to one of Chrissie's peonies or a bed of hostas. The key was to keep walking until you eventually arrived at the source. You'd know you were there if you reached a glassy porch, for inside it there were secateurs, gardening gloves, notes telling delivery vans to leave parcels and a 'please ring' sign. MacQueen and Woodside were two well-established artists. MacQueen's work was abstract, exploring the shape and colour seen when looking through a doorway or to a pool and they took you through this to another place. Woodside's work reminded me of a tapestry: a weft of colour and a weave of life, but now I realised they were like the paths of her garden. They lived here in the centre of Fife at the heart of a high-walled garden. I rang the bell.

Charlie, like me, had large fat feet which were unhappy to be crammed into shoes, and he shuffled around the house in sandals and socks. He was wearing painting clothes, probably all that was ever worn, and Chrissie was lively and full of smiles. There were two lurchers resting in dog baskets near the Aga and on the walls were photographs of grandchildren. Next to the kitchen was a large Victorian conservatory full of paintings and a twin set of easels, and next to this was their painting storeroom. The main living room was a riot of discarded projects, a computer and packing material. They had lived here so long that, while the garden grew around them becoming ever richer, so did the house. It was an artistic ecosystem easily disturbed by visiting art dealers. I asked Charlie what his work was about.

'I don't really know, Tony. I've been doing them for fifty years and I'm still not sure. Something inspires me and I work on a composition until I'm happy with it.'

'It's very intuitive?'

'Yes, I sort of make them up.'

'Makey-uppy?'

'What? Makey-uppy? That's not even a word.'

Chrissie's newest work was laid out in another room. Six winter scenes with dogs, crows and the Lomond Hills leaned against the wall and the black marble mantlepiece. Her work had become increasingly sought-after. The paintings were alive. She didn't talk about them: just painted. Chrissie disappeared outside to walk the dogs, leaving by a secret entrance. I headed north to visit another artist, Alan Macdonald, with a stack of paintings in the Saab. Charlie helped pack, and then waved me off. 'Makey-uppy,' he muttered as he shook his head.

★

There are too many paintings in most large society exhibitions. Shows with easily confused acronyms: RSA, RA, RGA, VAS, SSC, PI – and many of the silver-framed works on show are by the familiar old guard, so I always move through them quickly, waiting to be stopped by something new. Alan Macdonald's large canvas was one of these. Exquisitely painted figures in a tin bath: the artist as a cardinal with paint brushes in his hand, a lady in a blue dress with one strap down. There was a sphinx, a pot of dried flowers, a miniature Parthenon and a black sagging sail behind them, while they were pulled through the large canvas by a rope. There were words, letters, numbers and riddles too. These were devices to catch you, an alchemist's joke, but what absorbed me most was the composition. It was an image that Macdonald had reshaped until everything was in balance, like a tower of cards. He had then removed a card and captured the tower before it fell. It was dynamic. You could see that the blue-dressed lady had a plan and the cardinal-artist had no control at all. It was spellbinding but I ignored it. I was already showing work by another Allan MacDonald, Allan-the-Landscape.

Two Al(l)an Macd(D)onalds would be confusing. The next month I saw another painting by him. This time it was small, just a portrait of a man eating a crisp. He wore a strange hat, with an odd, pinned-back collar on his shirt. So small, but yet captivating. It was time, I realised, to meet the artist.

'Welcome.' I got out of my black Saab. I had squeezed through a narrow gate and entered the back garden of Alan Macdonald's large stone house. It was once the main bank in this seaward-facing town, and now the old banking space had been converted into a large studio, while the rest of the house sat around it, immaculate. He was not what I expected: a few years older than me, wearing a crisp shirt with black jeans and shoes. His wife, Carolynda, was close by. I was ushered through to his white painting space like a visiting ambassador. There were no works on the floor and no stacks of empty canvas waiting to be given life. Everything was on the wall and most were already in Macdonald's self-designed black frames. It was the most controlled studio I have seen.

'I need to see them like this, complete. Sometimes it's like whoa, what have I done, this is great: or I'll put it aside and rework it later. What do you think of this one – *The Rebirth of Venus*.'

It was hard not to notice a wall-sized, Rembrandt-dark canvas that would sit well within any national gallery.

'It's not what Venus expected. She's irritated. Damn it. But she's doing her best. The town's too small,' he laughed. 'The band is just two old guys making terrible music and the cardinal is selling tickets to the event. He's disappointed too, and she's been chaperoned by a prudish lady in a small dinghy sponsored by Coca Cola. I'm worth more than this, she thinks.' Alan changed his voice and gestures with the punchline. 'This is not what it was like last time.'

'It rocks, Alan. Everything in here rocks,' I said. 'How long do you spend doing it? It must take forever to work like this.'

'Oh, we're never out of here. We come in first thing and work into the night and, on occasion, we see a band or something. The rest of the time is spent here.' Carolynda had a small studio attached, where she painted old-fashioned sweets reflected on a mirrored surface. By 2020 these had developed into incredible scenes with jewelled birds and fantastical landscapes. The two of them lived mostly on the ground floor, painting, rarely knowing what would step into their work next.

'It's a playground,' he told me.

*

Eventually, the search for lost Scottish artists led me so far south that ozone and light filled the red van's cabin. It was

2015, and I missed a motorway turn-off and arrived at the Channel. Inland from here was Janette Kerr's southern studio. It was in an old barn and the land around was rich with hedges, trees and well-dressed riders on horses. I asked two schoolchildren in jodhpurs directions, as I was lost again. To me the south seemed dense, entangling, like a rabbit hole. Janette Kerr was small and energetic as she rushed to complete paintings. Her studio was already full of large foaming sea canvases that would soon sit in a sell-out one-person London exhibition. We talked of only three things – the north, paint, and the sea. 'Ten days. Only ten days until I'm in Shetland again.' She glanced north and smiled. 'I would live and paint there full time if I could.'

Like Turner, Janette Kerr had strapped herself to a ship's mast in a storm. The power of wind and wave called to her, and it was not easy for Janette to leave this briny tug. Her regular seas were in the north, and she captured these – from around Iceland and Shetland – arguably better than anyone else. I planned to bring these works north again, where they belong. 'Next time,' I said, 'we'll meet in Shetland.' I never told her that I hadn't quite made it that far. It was a long way, even from Inverness.

I left, and the red van headed first to a sculptor near Hay-on-Wye. I was so reliant on the satnav that I crossed the Severn Bridge and never realised that I had entered

Wales; or that I had left it as I headed towards Yorkshire with two forged iron dogs strapped in the back. Technology is borderless and it never stops. It would have been good to have stayed longer.

My destination was Eoghan Bridge, known for his sculptures of horses and riders. We'd met the previous year, when he and his father arrived in the gallery wearing kilts and speaking with strong Yorkshire accents. His father, who was head of sculpture at Edinburgh College of Art, had a physique that had forgotten to fade as he approached his mid-eighties; it bodied an increasingly forgetful mind with strong muscle and clean bright eyes. Eoghan was the same. Like most sculptors, he was used to hard work. I arrived in the Yorkshire ex-mining town as the kids came out of school. There were no riding boots and jodhpurs here, but hand-me-down uniforms with brightly coloured cheap trainers. In the shop opposite Eoghan's house were orange hand-cut discount signs in the shape of stars. The last coal mine had closed just over ten years before, and the town struggled to redefine itself.

'Yes, I've done equestrian sculpture for forty years now, Tony. Maybe too long, but I came back t'it. I'm a bit sick of galleries to tell the truth. Of always being pushed to a corner and then they only show the same thing. It's all 'bout money really. Y'must look at m'drawings too: m'fresh ideas.'

Eoghan Bridge turns things upside down. In his sculpture the horse was on top of the rider – a humorous play on man and beast's needs. As he pushed his work into new places, the gallery system pushed it back again – always to the same figure sitting crouched on top of a blue horse. All of Eoghan's work was slip cast (liquid clay poured into a mould, dried, treated and fired.) It was delicate, precise and labour-intensive. 'So much time, for so little,' he told me. Eoghan was sensitive and the world outside his front door was unjust and hard: especially in the art world. 'They're great,' I told him, and they were. 'Keep experimenting. I like the weird stuff too, maybe more. Keep turning it upside down, Eoghan. They'll come around.' He sold everything when it arrived north.

★

Kilmorack Gallery's stable of artists grew. New blood was a way to guard against a rapidly turning world. In some ways it was exciting: changing and reinventing things for a post bank-crash world where everything was gradually shifting. Now in 2020 I wander barefoot to the computer and change the music to Vivaldi and check for emails while I am there. It is a compulsion to click the email button now there is no one at the door.

Dog Food Days 2

The first dog food days were always seasonal. They could be survived with baked potatoes, dim bulbs and practical skills. They were predictable. Winter came and could be waited out, but now, after 2008, survival was about people. In the gallery, when the Nile stops flooding, you appreciate regulars more than ever.

Some, I am sure, were aware of how much of a lifeline they were; they would casually mention at the end of a long discussion about life, almost as a parting gesture, that they would like to make several purchases, and I would act surprised and unconcerned every time. 'Och Ian. No. There's really no need. Your house is full already.' But they would always buy. This is how you survive a plague or a banking crash that changes rhythms; you need friends and clients to rebuild a new predictable structure now the seasons have gone.

By the time of the banking crash I had already known many clients for thirteen years. The art teacher who first brought groups of schoolchildren to the gallery, who was the same size as the children that formed a miniature army with her at the front, always bought what she could with her teacher's salary and never missed a preview.

There was a man from Orkney, from the island of Hoy. Like the old camper van he drove, bits were starting to fall off him: bumpers, eyesight, wing mirrors and hearing, but he would always leave with something. He drove off with one particularly large painting in the van and that night, before catching the morning ferry to Orkney, he slept under the van while the painting remained inside. Tirsh, who drove through the night from Stratford and slept in the gallery's car park, also bought large amounts of work with her vicar's pension. The gallery could not have survived without these devoted clients.

There was David, an intelligent and aesthetic lawyer. Another gallery had been rude to him and now he bought from Kilmorack instead: painting upon painting. He always apologised for taking up my time and before leaving he would say 'I would like . . .' this or that. He was both buying beauty and helping it survive. It was not theoretical help, but real, especially in an economic wasteland. There were other clients too who, like David, became so regular they were like friends or family, appearing when the chips were down. New ones appeared, like Ann, a global citizen. She lived in Brazil with her tech-wizard husband before returning to Scotland when he died too young. Ann was both an intellect and an art collector. Just up the hill from the gallery was Anne-Mary. She only appeared when the gallery was at its most quiet and left with a small painting to sustain the gallery, like seeds on a bird table. As the years passed, a new ecology grew, a rich ecosystem of clients, friends and artists. I never saved money for dog food days but just curated this evolving habitat. The more complex and folded it became, the more stable it felt, but faith was always needed: waiting for the next unexpected sale.

The Inevitability of Connection is Evident

Kapka has gathered the tips of the first nettles and turned them into fritters. We eat them outside in the weak March sun. 'Sometimes, I'd like to go off-grid,' she says. 'I get too many emails. There's a pressure to do things, and I don't need it anymore.' My phone vibrates with a message and I disappear into the garden-shudy to reply.

My garden-shudy is small and warm, with a long, low window that looks over a field of sheep and beyond to the new pylons and an empty space where a few weeks before stood a forest. I built it the previous year, and here I am connected, 4G-ed, to everywhere, sending stories that would once have taken years to send. A story told by a painting disappears into the new grid – dismantled, reassembled and judged by algorithms. There are many stories and art should tell them.

★

Some tales have now ended. I change clothes in a discreet doorway. Half-naked in the London spring. Black shirt and tie, boots and scratchy kilt. That is all that is required. This is Gerald Laing's second service. The first was in a large marquee in the castle's garden up north. His stone pyramid was for the first time under canvas, and is now indoors, but it still points upwards, inseminating the stars, and around this there is a sea of tartan bodies. Gerald was writing a memoir before he died – a thousand pages long and brimful of tales. Boy-to-army, army-to-art, success, rejection, and success again, and now to death. It is a story well owned. I enter the London church with my kilt old and messy; Highland-style. Everyone else is in black suits. There is a contralto singing solo baroque like a sexless angel. Gerald's London life, of clubs and connections, is another story, another grid. After the service I spot another messy kilt at the back. It is Gus, Gerald's gardener. Gus is around five foot tall, but stocky and rough, with a love of booze and women. He is weeping more than anyone here. I see the family of Elizabeth Cameron the botanical painter too. She died a few years earlier. This time a large marquee is erected over a cherry tree in the garden, enbubbling its blossom. Kapka arrives from her meeting and I hear someone say to her, 'I like to sit hidden in the garden and write poetry. It connects me.'

'To what?'

'To what is important.'

My grandmother's funeral was not long before too,

her coffin lowered into the ground. 'In the sweat of thy face shalt thou eat bread, till thou return unto the ground; for out of it wast thou taken: for dust thou art, and unto dust shalt thou return.' The inevitability of connection is evident. Ultimately, we all re-grid.

★

My garden-shudy is so small that any breeze snuffs its warmth, like blowing out a candle, but today I let it find equilibrium with the outside. The cold is awakening, helping focus when I try to look under the hood of the gallery's website, at its connections. It is easy to be distracted by birdsong as I look at the slow-moving, mythological figures that describe the internet's algorithms. Authority (both page and domain), inbound links (discovered and lost) and crawling issues (URLs, tags, titles and all sorts of code) are mixed into a mystery soup that search engines judge. They check that the page functions correctly and from here it is a popularity contest. There are the greatest storytellers – *The New York Times*, the BBC. If they like your story and link to your website, you rise up rankings significantly and are seen by many. If a little website – an artist, a directory – likes your story and links to you, you rise a little. And so the most liked tales ascend. If people don't like it, and quickly leave the website, it falls. This algorithm was devised twenty-five years earlier, just as Black Allan first opened the door of the old kirk to me, and now it is everywhere, marrying popularity with (domain) authority and power. Kilmorack Gallery's website is clearly the best around, but deserves more authority. It is harder in a remote area to get your story told, and this is what the new virtual world measures. In cyberspace you either consume stories or make them. I leave to fix the gallery's spring. The internet's world is too abstract for me today. Their numbers are not real, and it is pleasant to be outside. I off-grid for a while.

The spring itself with its stone surround has always flowed, but the large nineteenth-century cistern into which it flows has a crack, so the water level has dropped, reducing the gallery tap's flow to a trickle. It stops completely when a frog enters the pipe. They were always here, small and unseen in the dark. I have not inspected it for twenty years, and back then I had help from two crazy hippies – Bodo and Nick. Shifting the two large stone slabs that cap the spring is a daunting task so I have been putting it off. It will need to be drained too and I have never figured out a clever solution. The answer is that it is not clever. Fixing a spring is practical, wet and strenuous. It is an immersive experience. I set off wearing waders, with buckets and a large metal rod to help shift the stones. It is the same walk I made twenty years before, but now with grey beard, long hair and increased bulk. It was a fun day back then; in the sun, struggling to remove the capping stone, laughing when Bodo crawled into the cold spring water in his underwear. These three skinny ghosts still haunt the spring as I slide the stone caps with ease. Twenty years of shifting paintings has only added to my strength and now I am armed with waders too. I climb in. The water is high, pushing against my body and lowering with every bucket down towards the silt, gravel and frogs. There are so many down here, and I wonder if they have always lived below, looking up at the crack between the two capping stones, or if they have fallen in. I encourage them with wet hands into a box and lift them out into the world. The rest is up to them. And then I too arise from the cistern baptised.

'Aye, Tony. Another three parcels for you,' Brian says as I waddle back in my waders. 'It's good to do something physical,' he expands when he sees the wet state of me. 'Good to be alive.'

'Busy, Brian?'

'Aye, it's like Christmas. Everyone's at home on their computers buying things online. It's strange. I drop a parcel off and don't see anyone. Maybe a face at the window. You seem busy.'

'Aye, it's busy right enough.'

One box has been sent from the Isle of Harris. It is

packed with the precision of an engineer, and the cut polystyrene whooshes as it is removed. Inside, wrapped in an old shirt that is still encrusted with plaster and dust, is a large piece of carved black Harris stone, and inside this stone is a vial of deep ocean water, pinned in place with whalebone and brass. It is a Steve Dilworth Drogue: more of a magical object than conventional sculpture. I tried for years to get Steve Dilworth's work but for a long time he was tied to another gallery. Things are different now. His old gallery is gone, and Steve is happy to send work from his island studio to Kilmorack when able. It seems a long time now since our last visit: Kapka, Globbie and I, on the early morning winter ferry.

*

From Kilmorack the quickest way to Harris is to catch the Ullapool boat to Lewis. It was November and the ferry was quiet, just us and the big glass forward-facing window, a slow sway and the hum of the motor. I remember all ferry journeys and forget most car trips. They punctuate travel. The day never brightened as we drove south from Stornoway. Harris and Lewis are landscapes mostly of rock with a thin veneer of vegetation and beautiful beaches where the body of the island has been ground down to sand by Atlantic waves. Here, at the western edge of

Europe, nature still dwarfs man. Steve Dilworth's house and studio were not what I expected. They nestled just off the road, almost into the hill. It was not far to the sea: over a short wooden fence, across the single-track road and down the rocky slope to Geocrab bay. This was where much of Steve Dilworth's sculptural material came from. Either dragged down from the hill or carried up from the shore: wood, stone and the occasional carcass. Steve was tall, with charismatic, prominent features. 'Please, please. Come in.'

The domestic side of the cottage was bright and clean, like a small chapel furnished with books and sculpture. 'This is where I eat, rest and think. And this is where I work.' Steve opened the door to his workshop. Opposite us was a freezer where dead things were kept, waiting for reanimation, and there were bones and stones in piles. On the workbench was an object – a bird-like body of carved and polished rosewood with feathers fashioned from found and beaten nails, and inside this, a mummified woodcock. Steve picked it up so we could see the bird's beak poking through a slit. Beneath this its dried body rested. 'They joke that no one is safe in here.' I saw a spark in Steve's eye as he glanced towards the chest freezer. It is easy to become fanatical about his work: offerings and connections to bigger things, beyond our tiny human lifespans. Death is part of everything and Steve Dilworth had spent the last forty years here, designing and crafting power objects. It would be easy to lose sanity at the edge of Europe where the land cuts off into the sea. It was dim and grey outside and the air was remote-island air. Kapka looked towards me. She prefers places with trees and wide-flowing rivers like home. This studio was a personal place. It was behind the iconostas, a place for priests, and we left.

Dinner began with seaweed freshly gathered from below the cottage, followed by curry with herbs and spices sent from India.

'She thought I said Paris when I suggested moving here,' he joked.

Joan smiled politely. She had heard this before. 'I like to visit cities sometimes, to dress up and eat out. Next month we see Booker T and the MGs in Ronnie Scott's. It's a birthday treat. But Harris provides everything. It is amazing what drifts here. There's a direct current from America.'

'The geology is incredible too. There's such a feeling of ancientness: bedrock and bog,' I commented.

'Yes, I love the rock. I call it Harris stone but it is really dunite: four billion years old, from a time when Harris was south of the equator. It's difficult to conceive, and hard to work, so resistant, but it connects with this distance; and it is so close. Just a difficult drag down the hill. Harris sometimes feels like a place without time. I was planning to bury my hanging figure, the one from human bones, out in the bog so it could be dug up in the future. A riddle for whoever comes next. But now it's in Chicago.'

'It must have taken a year to make. So much time and work just to bury it.'

'And more. I learned so much. Preserving meat, re-fleshing bone, binding seagrass. An offering has to involve a sacrifice, or it doesn't mean anything. You must give an object of significance.'

Dilworth's work was not morbid jokes or riddles. It was about remembering and connecting to what lies outside our quick lives. The craftsmanship was part of it. It was a way of investing an object with prayerlike magic. The next morning we were waved off, and we drove a circuit around the island. I had been here once before. Back then, we knocked on a crofter's door to use the phone. There were two generations in the small sitting room and only the smallest amount of English spoken. They fed us white bread and butter and looked on smiling, discussing us in Gaelic.

★

The second box in the gallery contains three watercolour and ink drawings by Robert Powell. The first shows one of the horsemen of the apocalypse followed by his band of demons, the second a tower of naked and grotesque bodies hiding from a plague doctor, and the third is a retelling of the annunciation. Robert Powell is a storyteller: a young fogey, either buried in books or working in single-haired detail on a drawing.

'You must see the new studio. We can meet there. Phone me from George IV Bridge and I'll let you in.'

This was my first meeting with Robert Powell and I parked outside Edinburgh's Chambers Street museum and walked the short distance to our rendezvous: past cafés and libraries with the occasional dark drop to the Cowgate below. These were old haunts from student days. Edinburgh is a city of secrets. One night and three of us, already tipsy, were led from a small folk pub into a town building, down a trapdoor, and below into an unlit buried street. We were told it had been closed due to the plague. Our guide had acquired keys to this secret, and there were rumours of other passages too, but those keys were kept more securely.

Robert Powell was tall, with a thin body buried under a fat scarf and hat. He was like one of his drawings: long fingers, long feet and tufts of misplaced hair. He was standing beside a giant-sized, slightly open door, which he closed and locked when I entered. 'It is too large for me,' he said as I was led up a grand marble staircase to the first circular landing. We looked up to a glass dome far above and to the four identical empty circular landings which layered the ascent. 'The top floor is the best,' so we trudged upwards, leaving footprints in the dust and plaster.

There were ten rooms on each floor and we looked into some as we climbed upwards, past ornate plasterwork, high ceilings and windows that looked down on the now-small red buses. Eventually we were at the top. Robert had a small table set up with a magnifying glass, pencils and ink. 'It is really very silly working from here. So big and so cold, and my work isn't large. My hands seize sometimes too. But let me show you this.' We climbed out of a window, past gargoyles, and below us were the rooftops of Edinburgh. We were the same height as the castle: two mother trees in a forest, but this one was invisible. 'I like it here, high up. This building goes another seven storeys down, as far as the Cowgate, but it is too creepy to enter.'

'Should we take a quick look?' I suggested.

He shakes his head. 'There are trapdoors and unopened rooms. I can't go there.'

It was incredible that a building this size could remain hidden.

We headed back to the room with his latest work. It was a series of twelve etchings inspired by fantastical human projects: a self-devouring supermarket, an erotic party set in an outer realm of hell, the *School of Ikaros*, a ladder to heaven that can't be climbed, the naming of the beasts, the hypnotic power of technology, an elevated poet. Robert looked upwards to the stars too, and overseas, and down the hill to the National Gallery, a place of forgetting. We returned outside and sat with the gargoyles. From this building we could see so much, like a camera obscura or a panopticon; and the building itself looked up through its glass dome towards heaven, while below there was a labyrinth of hells too frightening to enter. Once births and deaths were registered here: the start and end of every story in the region. Robert knew all of this and, with the library next door too, he would never run out of parables. But this building was a ruin and its stories now dust.

The giant door closed as we left, and we had a coffee in a café down the street. It was in a room that came off this building. 'Have you ever explored?' I asked the owner.

He shook his head and looked towards an old door. 'No,' he replied. 'It is insanely scary through there.'

*

Today in Kilmorack, Robert Powell's three plague works need framing. He has just married, in a service that no one other than himself and the bride knew about (their parents thought it was just lunch) and now they have a rapidly growing baby. 'Like a maggot,' I said.

'Yes, that's what we call him.'

And there are more stories than ever now. Even in one Edinburgh street. I'd agreed to take the three paintings along with some other works to be framed.

Framing is not easy. It takes a certain eye, which is why I go to Ruaridh-the-Frame. It is not for his speed.

Ruaridh-the-Frame and the North

November, 2019

The drive to Ullapool is always beautiful, especially with the ridges of An Teallach in the distance. For many years I played loud trip hop in the car when driving this road, towards rainbows and hills but never reaching them. Now I drive in silence and let thoughts come and go. Last time, it must have been a trick of the eye, a bird igniting my vision, but I swear I saw a Second World War bomber flying low with a crewman leaning out of an open door waving. I must have been dreaming. Ruaridh would have said that the fabric is thin in places, especially now. He is a biker, an axe thrower and a rock and country singer. He sees aliens and his beard dwarfs mine. If on his motorbike, to avoid accidents he ties it with a rubber band and tucks it into his jacket. 'Logos have become like religious symbols,' he told me. 'They are a dark magic, so ingrained into the way we think that we are not free.'

A frame is something that tethers a painting to a spot. It takes it from the artist's easel into someone else's life. Ruaridh is the unlikely midwife of many paintings.

Wiping it down and presenting it swaddled to its new parents. This is why I go to him. He cares.

'I struggled to get the frame right for the Russian artist,' he says. 'so I walked and looked at the hills and moss for inspiration. Nothing came, until I lay on a stone and concentrated on my breath and then bam it hit me. Now what have you got for me?'

We discuss the new works and their frames. The big Paul Bloomers are a challenge. They are massive woodcuts of birds seen above Shetland. In Bloomer's prophetic vision the birds connect to what is important, and a small figure underneath looks up and listens. They are two metres long and require glass. 'That'll be £100 each.'

'But the glass and backing board alone will cost that.'

'Well, maybe £200 each.'

'Lets say for now £250, or you'll be losing money.'

This is why Ruaridh is so slow at framing. He charges so little that his guillotine blades go blunt, but that is not what he is connected to. He, like Paul Bloomer, listens and waits.

'Hey, you're a groovy guy, Ruaridh. Kapka thinks it would be good to go off-grid for a while. What do you reckon?'

'Well, Tony, there are many grids and webs out there. Maybe we need to choose which ones to join. It's not just buying a turbine. I look out for signs and follow them.

That's my grid.'

'And axe throwing, aliens, golf, country music, acting and framing. You spread yourself a wee bit thin Ruaridh.'

'Yes, but I am me.' He goes in for a dog-like hug. 'I'll see you when I'm done.'

I know it will be a long wait.

★

There are more rainbows than ever as I drive east, and the heather glows golden in the low light. Looking for signs, Ruaridh said. That is what brought me here, to this beautiful place. I've always followed them, heading a little north each time. That is what an artist should do too, feel their way. Sometimes it is north. It can be hard to look away, like staring into a fire.

The North

Scotland disappears as the ferry leaves Aberdeen. We are heading north to Shetland. But north is relative. Not far from the ferry terminal is the studio of Ade Adesina. Aberdeen is a long way north of his birthplace in Nigeria, but he has settled where ferries only head upwards, still further: to the Northern Isles.

'Thank you for coming, Tony, and welcome, Kapka.' We are led into his studio where two-metre high, black-framed linocuts are stacked. There is a wall where ongoing work is pinned, an easel, and a sofa to sleep on when nothing can drag Ade away from here. 'This is what I am working on.'

In front of us is a red lino board. Every millimetre has been carved to reveal a post-now world. It is a prayer where a cosmic tree and the music of the spheres sing life into the earth. At the top of the unfinished board are three planets, hanging like orbiting leaves, and at the root is the grounding trunk of a giant baobab tree. Saxophones, sunflowers and seahorses with wings swim through the centre. There are clocks too, tick-tocking the countdown.

'I get inspiration from everywhere. You know. I put

everything into it: from Nigeria, Aberdeen, everything. It's easy to be angry, so I'm trying to step back, become a spectator, and now maybe find a way forward.'

I have loved Ade's ecological themes – trees, whales and changing water levels – since he appeared in the art world four years before. I feel Ade jumping ahead, switched on, and constantly thinking of new ideas. Being here, in the studio, pulls him back down to the now. It earths him through the hours of carving and the technical precision of printing. Discipline makes his visions tangible and vital. We agree a show and decide to call it 'New Leaves'. I forget to ask him why he has remained so far north. Maybe he can hear more, where it is quieter, away from the chatter.

The boat gently rocks for twelve hours to Lerwick. It is off season, so our fellow passengers are mostly locals: shopping, attending funerals or back from urgent hospital visits in Scotland that are missed if the ferry is forced to turn back. Orkney is windy, a home to cows and ancient stones. It is an island of farmers. Shetland is not like this. It is windier still, and instead of cows there are salt-and-hurricane-proof Shetland sheep. Locals are boat people, fishermen and, since the 1970s, oil workers too. We drive off the ferry onto this impossible rock, park, and gale-puff through the door of a small café for a bowl of soup and a bacon roll. Inside it is cosy and I see myself in a mirror.

I have aged back to the thirteenth century with red face, and hair and beard backcombed by the wind into a fat nest. I taste the water that drips from me. It is slightly salty.

I am surprised to find a parking ticket stuck onto the windscreen of our red van, but this blows away as soon as the transparent sleeve is opened. We look as it flies across the car park, over the harbour and far out to sea. Here, the old gods have the last word. Next stop is south to our hotel, which sits looking out to the sea as everything does here. The air inside is clean and cold, even in the wardrobe and under the sheets. It is midday and the island is full of sea-scrubbed light. Even when darkness comes three hours from now, the air will remain rich with oxygen and minerals. Somehow, there is more of it than back home in Scotland. The beer and food – lamb or fish – are surprisingly good at night, and the craic in the pub makes it worth sitting on the tall stools until closing time. I am told that this is not Scotland, and that winter is long, so it is good to have a project. For some it is making reproduction Viking costumes for Up-Helly-Aa. Summer, they say, is very different. The time of simmer dim, when it never really gets dark. The old gods are hard to ignore here.

Our first visit is to Gail Harvey, who lives alone in a cottage, its roof tied down with rope and wire. Her work is large with the colours and patterns seen from her window; patchworked together in abstract oil paint. The bold marks used, big arching brush strokes and scumbling dripping paint journeys, come from places that even Gail doesn't understand.

'I hope you like oatcakes. Shetland makes some of the best oatcakes,' she says as we are welcomed in. There is a studio next door, which extends into the house where her work is pinned to walls and stored under beds. Everything is painted white to make the most of the light and Gail drifts from one work to another looking for something lost.

'I see them as music. The rhythm and energy of this place is a song. Maybe I overwork them sometimes. What do you think? Would you like another oatcake?'

The studio is an island within an island.

'It's not always like this outside. Today is blue and still, but sometimes it's mental. After a westerly gale, I need to clean seaweed from the window or it sticks and leaves marks.'

The sea is three fields from her home. 'Wouldn't it be possible to plant trees?'

She has thought about this. The seaweed is a problem. 'No, salt and wind stops them growing. Maybe graduated would work: a moss to a shrub, to a bush, to a tree. Weisdale has some trees.'

As in the hotel, air follows us around, but here it is more ghostly, more corporeal than ever.

'And it can be lonely here, just painting. But it is a compulsion. I can never leave.'

★

The following day we meet Ruth Brownlee. Her house is very different from Gail's. It is low down, almost touching the fizz of pebble, wave and foam which sings just a few metres from her door. This beach is part of a circle that forms a bay, and at its entrance a theatre of light and waves plays out as dusk approaches. This show is the subject of Ruth's paintings. We knock, open and shout 'hello'. White horses catch the last light before the dark-blue-ink sky turns black.

'You must be Tony.'

'And Kapka,' I add.

We enter a warm space full of a child's toys, an easel and paints. It is like being welcomed into a shorebird's nest, so low down and cosy.

'I am always busy. Galleries want my work and they sell.' She smiles at the full order book. 'But there's not much time for reflection.' Her daughter shows Kapka around her room as Ruth and I talk about sizes and frames. Outside, night almost closes a curtain on its show, but not quite. The moon is still there.

★

Peter Davis lives in the centre of the island, Weisdale, the only place with trees, and I have looked forward to seeing them for Shetland, like Iceland and other northern places, once had woodland before it was cut for firewood and cleared for sheep. I have left Kapka in the hotel to shelter from the buffeting wind. Peter lives in the hamlet's former manse.

'You know, Tony, this old house isn't right for me. It's just me here. There's drips and draughts, constant things, distractions.'

It is winter and I hardly notice the small, bare trees outside.

'I'll move towards the sea if the opportunity comes my way. That's why I am here, the sea.'

He leads me to his studio, which is more of a home to him than the large rambling house. Here, there are no distractions. It is a place of control, full of brushes, pigment and drying paper, and lights so he can work into the night.

'Stones are my secret. They let me tilt the board so I can control the water and pigment with the smallest adjustments and let it sit until ready. I spend a lot of time looking at paint dry.'

When working, Peter Davis is no longer a Yorkshire-born ex-teacher, he is a Zen master. The

Shetland world of water and rock harmonises with mindful breath. I envisage him working, the large house and scrawny trees dissolving as he slowly lays water and pigment down, breathing out with every brushstroke. Peter's focus has become a compulsion, a connection to something bigger.

I drive back to the hotel.

'It is strange,' Kapka says. 'All three artists live alone after moving here with a partner. It was meant to be the perfect escape. Both Gail and Ruth's men died young. Let's not move here.'

I can picture life in the far north, side by side with the old wild gods, but that will not happen. The only commercial gallery we found is Vaila Gallery, run by Dorota Rychlik. The wood-lined interior was salvaged from her castle on Vaila, her own island, and she commutes from it daily. On the day we met her, she had to row to the main island because the motor wouldn't start. Once a year she drives to Poland to pick apples from her family's garden. This is what it takes to survive on Shetland, cold boat crossings and long journeys for fruit. I could never be as tough as Dorota.

★

We have one more visit to make before catching the ferry home, but it is hard to meet up in person. He is either teaching in college until late or leaving his studio early. In the summer he fishes and walks, and in the winter he works. We mention his name to the bearded, traditionally woollen-jumpered man, geanied, whom we have befriended at the bar, and he goes misty-eyed. 'Paul Bloomer,' he slurs. 'Paul Bloomer. I love hus work. I try tae see hus shows when they're ane in Lerwick. They're incredible. I'd love a peerie piss, somedae.' The barman nods too. 'A small piece,' he translates. Everyone here likes Paul Bloomer's work. I'm not sure if it is the giant woodcuts of birds they admire, or the giant Bosch-like drinking scenes. It could be both. We eventually enter Paul Bloomer's studio alone. He can't make it. 'I'm sorry, Tony. The studio is open. Just let yourself in and you can see all my latest paintings and drawings there. I'm sorry I can't make it but thank you very much for trying.'

It is mid-afternoon when we arrive and already almost dark. We can see St Ninian's Island further down the hill. To explore it in the gloom would not be safe. It is an old place, like Kilmorack, with a spirit and a history that goes back to the earliest times, before the Vikings and Christians, to the Neolithic. Paul's studio is in a large agricultural outbuilding that looks down over the island. Its high, windowless walls hold back most of the wind, but some enters through the tiniest gaps, the ever-present breath of Shetland. Work is everywhere, arranged in different projects. Small colour studies are pinned to the wall in one corner, and in another giant canvases are constantly pondered over and added to. Above another table are small drawings he plans to turn into a series of etchings – 'The Return of the Light' followed by another, 'Entering the Dark'. There are a lot of circles in Paul's work that make a geometry, a door, an eye, that leads elsewhere, and for him this portal rarely closes.

Museum-sized paintings from past exhibitions are in the centre of the room with rolled canvases resting on top. We are never quite alone: the wind rattles the door and Paul's empty shape, remembered by a survival suit, hangs martyred from a hook above us. It is a double haunting: from an absent artist and from the ancient island below.

'It feels wrong to be here without him,' Kapka comments. 'Like entering his head.' We pull out a large drawing.

'This is what an artist should do,' I say. 'They must have a story and Paul Bloomer's never stop coming. It takes a sort of nakedness.'

There are some harsh tales too. We unwrap a woodcut that shows neglected horses starving in a field and another is of unemployed men, drinkers. He made these in the industrial Midlands just as I opened the gallery. Back then, factory workers in his hometown stamped metal or dipped things in terrible chemicals, those that still had jobs. He did this too for a while, until an unavoidable poetry rose in him, filling his sail, and blowing north. The wind is protecting this place. It likes him and doesn't want us to linger, so we leave and drive back silent in the dark. It is our last night on Shetland.

In the morning it is windier still. Flights are cancelled and our ferry rocks even as it lies in its Lerwick berth. Kapka insists on buying a large supply of Shetland oatcakes, smoked salmon and cheese, and we walk Globbie one last time on the clifftop, parking the red van head to wind so the doors don't blow off, and crawling along the ground when we get out. 'It's on,' Kapka tells me. 'I've had a text and we still sail tonight.' We are soon on *MV Hamnavoe* where wet towels are placed over the tables so plates don't slip off. That is for the brave or foolhardy. Most, if they have a cabin, enter it and do not leave when it is like this.

An hour into the voyage and it is difficult to stand. We rock and slide down waves. I look out the cabin window and one moment the sea is miles off, a distant landscape, and at the next it is just outside the porthole, staring at me: wave-to-eye and eye-to-wave. There was too much cheese with the oatcakes. I dream. I always do on a boat at sea.

The North

Dreams

We are running in the dream. Our bodies are no more than circles with matchstick legs. I look to amoeba-Kapka and help her to higher ground with my matchstick arms. Below is a desert of flooded or burning buildings, quarries and pylons. Occasionally bushes ignite around us, so we run further, quickly, on short legs. We run past Ruaridh-the-Frame. In the dream he is a bear talking to small balls of light and he nods a greeting as we pass. Eventually we reach a hillside where abandoned tents have been pitched. It is a familiar place from an earlier dream. There is one rock, higher than others, and we climb on top of it with our small bodies and find a nest deep in its moss. It is cosy in the warm ground.

The next thing I am aware of is growing upwards, like a bulb towards the light. Life fills me, pushing my extremities up and out, uncurling hands and fingers, pushing my man's form out. I am naked and erect on top of the rock. My fresh green face and body feel the wind, salty and scrubbed, and my head slowly rotates. A perfect note comes from my reborn mouth. This is me, a true self. I bend down and plunge my uncurled limbs into the ground and send a further signal down through rock and soil. Kapka now rises too. We are not alone. Our rooted feet tell us this.

I awaken briefly. The boat has pitched and slammed into a wave. It is two in the morning and the *Hamnavoe* hasn't moved position. We are stuck somewhere in the North Sea battling wind. I slip back into the dream.

The feeling is one of surging, a quickening, as life throbs through our rooted feet, using ancient pathways as it goes. Sometimes it is an energy that jumps from root to air, sprouting green as it lands, and in other moments it is gale-puffed upwards to where we have a better view. Kapka and I fly and twist together. From up high we see a leafing everywhere. There are others like us: rooted or hovering around doors of open energy, connecting to local spirits and letting others see the once-hidden deities too. We see Black Allan below, unchanged, gathering flowers. Tendrils of ivy and honeysuckle climb up pylons. Moss and trees reclaim buildings and quarries as old connections are re-made. Time speeds up, folds and circles back to its beginning and, below us, grey slowly brightens, to be replaced with the colours of artists' visions. A carapace of illusion lifts. The burst of energy, the perfect note is everywhere, seeding a new way. We see the world re-map and spin on its centre to come to rest on a new network.

Kapka turns over in the small bed. She too has drifted elsewhere and awakes with a moan. I look at the clock, and the ferry's position on the small screen hasn't changed for four hours. We are stuck in purgatory, between Shetland and Scotland. I slip off to a very different place.

It is tight in this suit. The tie and collar strangle my breath and I'm wearing underwear that clutches, squeezing in a dictator's grip. There are no rooms, just this airless corridor. I wander on, looking for a way out. Somewhere ahead I hear the sound of rocks being crunched and ground down, and a deep electrical throb. The world is out there, sealed off.

'Allan, Allan.' I have seen a figure and it is Allan 'the landscape' MacDonald, slowly moving in the shadows. He is as grey as me. There is no romper suit wiped with yellows and oranges, or baseball cap with Hebridean-sky blue. 'Where are we, Allan? What has happened? He walks on, disconnected, and I follow. Eventually, he turns around. 'They took us away from it. They stopped me looking and painting. They stopped us all.' He gestures to a small hole and I look through. There is nothing there, just a machine grinding rocks and another one buzzing. The sound grows louder and louder, until I awake drenched in sweat and dread.

Kapka is asleep, with arms crossed like a pharaoh. We still have not moved. We have been in the storm's grip for over ten hours. I stumble to the small toilet and wedge my knees against the wall to keep steady as the boat rocks.

I think that dream, the fear, has shrunk me. I pee and stumble back into our narrow bed. We must either move on or turn back, I think. I close my eyes and drift home, to Kilmorack, to the spring behind the gallery.

I feel different here. My legs are strong. Their sinew is warm and powerful as I extend each one in turn, and I stretch my long fat toes too. These feet have gripped and taught me about my small dark world. I open my eyes as I am carried upwards and out of the cistern that has been my home. I blink. It has never been so light. Like me, the world is green and brown, and the water flows over my back. I am baptised. A new life. I look back towards the dark cistern and forwards down the boggy slope towards the river, and I hop.

The *Hamnavoe* is moving forwards again and the new motion wakes us both. We land in Aberdeen at 8.30 a.m. where the air is somehow different. It tastes of granite and ploughed fields. With the rising sun behind us, we wester homewards, pulling over as soon as possible to feel the ground. Kapka turns to me, stares, and pulls a leaf from my hair. 'Strange.' She looks into my eyes. 'There are no trees on Shetland and it is winter.'

We drive on, through winter and onto spring. A very different spring. As the world rotates, art navigates. I am an art dealer. Like a beekeeper, I build a hive for their work.

Closing

That is my confession, dear spring, dear forest and dear river. We didn't mean to harm you. We just forgot many things. And some of us, sometimes, remembered.

Acknowledgments

Apologies to the people included in these confessions, for I have sketched events and characters in the briefest way and omitted so much. People mentioned are not themselves but archetypes, built from hazy memories, and I have enjoyed our journeys.

And apologies to the people not included. There are many artists missing because of the narrative: James Newton Adams, Paul Barnes, Shona Barr, Colin Brown, Patricia Cain, Fionna Carlisle, Sam Cartman, Duke Christie, Kate Downie, Joe Fan, Catherine Imhof-Cardinal, Janette Kerr, Liz Knox, Marian Leven, Madeline MacKay, Pinkie Maclure, Alan McGowan, Ann Oram, Carina Prigmore, Paul Reid, Iona Roberts, Beth Robertson Fiddes, Allison Weightman and Christopher Wood. There are stories in all of them too. Apologies also to people employed – especially Ruth Tauber and Georgina Coburn – and friends and family. But we are all connected.